BE
A
HERO!

BE
A
HERO!

THE ESSENTIAL SURVIVAL GUIDE TO ACTIVE-SHOOTER EVENTS

JOHN GEDDES AND **ALUN REES**

FOREWORD BY **DON MANN**

Skyhorse Publishing

Skyhorse Publishing books may be purchased in bulk at special discounts for sales promotion, corporate gifts, fund-raising, or educational purposes. Special editions can also be created to specifications. For details, contact the Special Sales Department, Skyhorse Publishing, 307 West 36th Street, 11th Floor, New York, NY 10018 or info@skyhorsepublishing.com.

Skyhorse® and Skyhorse Publishing® are registered trademarks of Skyhorse Publishing, Inc.®, a Delaware corporation.

Visit our website at www.skyhorsepublishing.com.

10 9 8 7 6 5 4 3

Library of Congress Cataloging-in-Publication Data is available on file.

Cover design by Rain Saukas
Cover photo credit: iStock

Print ISBN: 978-1-5107-2123-4
Ebook ISBN: 978-1-5107-2124-1

Printed in the United States of America

This book is dedicated to all the victims of active shootings.
Too many to name here; too few to forget.

Contents

Foreword

In *Be a Hero*, former SAS commando John Geddes and journalist and author Alun Rees offer a commonsense approach to the global epidemic of violent attacks on our society. The authors brilliantly outline in easy-to-understand yet comprehensive detail the threat of the active shooter and what steps should be taken to increase your chances of surviving an attack.

Although some folks in the military and law enforcement communities know how to react to an active shooter, the vast majority of people in the United States have never received this type of training. Now, thanks to John Geddes and Alun Rees, these principles can be readily understood by reading and understanding the guidelines presented in *Be a Hero*.

An active shooter usually tries to kill as many people as possible and will not stop until taken down. The victims are often attacked well before the police are able to respond. This is an essential fact. You cannot afford to simply wait for the police to arrive to save the day. Steps that can save your life—and the lives of your family and your coworkers—can and should be learned ahead of time.

A child, a student, a worker, or someone just waiting for a train—anyone could be at risk of an attack from an active shooter. *Be a Hero* was not written to scare the reader but to inform and educate.

Following the attacks on 9/11, I was asked to create an active-shooter training program for a federal agency and spent the next several years training government employees, law enforcement personnel, and civilians. Although we all understood the dangers involved with the active shooter at that time, I am stunned at just how much these attacks have increased over the past decade.

In the United States alone, there is now an average of almost two active-shooter attacks every month, and these attacks have occurred in more than forty of the fifty states. Globally, including the attacks that take place in war zones, the number is in the tens of thousands.

These attacks are not predictable, and in most cases the carnage took place in less than five minutes.

The FBI conducted a study of 160 active shooter incidents in which 486 innocent people were killed and another 557 wounded. In some of the attacks family members, former spouses, or cow-orkers were targeted; in others, it was just violent indiscriminate killing.

The FBI study revealed that in 21 of the 160 incidents, unarmed citizens—principals, teachers, and facility staff—bravely confronted the active shooter and disrupted the attacks.

Many of the active-shooter attacks happened in malls, schools, and businesses, but any place with a large gathering of people is a potential target.

These studies point out how real this threat is to our society, and they also highlight the importance of training—not only for our first responders but for all citizens.

As I always told my students, "Just imagine how you would feel, for the rest of your life, if an attack occurred that killed your family, friends, or coworkers, and you did not take the simple steps that could have saved those lives because you did not know what steps to take. Plan for the worst-case scenario and hope for the best."

I strongly believe that we all need to do our best to recognize and understand the threats we may face—and to remain vigilant, prepared, and ready to act if attacked. *Be A Hero* will better prepare you to survive the worst-case scenario.

Don Mann
Navy SEAL Team SIX (retired)

Preface

It will never happen to you, will it?

You're walking to work through a London street, sipping coffee in a Mumbai hotel or a Paris café. Maybe you're in the crowd at a marathon in Boston or studying in a high school at Columbine. All is peaceful, as it all should be. And then the gates of hell open. Windows implode; the physical impact of shock waves strikes you as a device explodes nearby. Whether or not you survive a bomb blast is a complete draw of the lottery. You are one of the lucky ones, but then the shooting begins and you hear the rattle of automatic gunfire coming your way. Terror takes hold of you. What do you do next? Which way do you turn, and who can you turn to?

In military terms you have, in effect, been ambushed—but you're a civilian. You've had none of the training that automatically kicks in when a soldier comes under attack. You've not been tested under fire. You don't understand the tactical nuances of the choices you next make.

Shock, fear, and hysteria will take over. You will not be prepared for decision making but you'll be faced with life-or-death choices as an active shooter picks victims at random.

I can help you. My name is John Geddes and I've written this guide to help you survive. It's designed as an aid for civilians in the event they are drawn into the chaos and terror of an active shooter event.

I've drawn on my extensive experience as a Special Air Service warrant officer on active duty alongside other elite troops. I took part in scores of anti-terror operations and covert interdictions around the globe, frequently with colleagues from US Delta Force. And as a young soldier fighting in the Falkland War, I had a sobering introduction to the realities of battlefield casualties.

I learned more when I left the Special Forces to pursue a career protecting TV crews, diplomats, and businessmen on perilous journeys into the insurgency and jihad of Iraq, Afghanistan, and Africa. I shepherded them through riots, bombings, and ambushes by gun and grenade.

Over the years, I've briefed hundreds of clients on how to react when danger presents. I can brief you too on how to best control the inevitable panic. I'll equip you with the tools needed to make lucid decisions in the midst of utter confusion and chaos.

It seems barely a week goes by without some new outrage unfolding on our television screens, and the numbers are increasing at a frantic rate.

The facts on this are stark. In 2010, fifteen terrorist attacks outside of war zones were recorded worldwide. By 2015, the numbers had rocketed to 118 separate atrocities. In the first three months of 2016 alone, twenty-five attacks occurred, including the destabilizing attacks on the Belgian capital, Brussels. By the end of the year, 432 people had been murdered, and hundreds more were injured, in terror attacks in the United States and Europe. This included the worst terror outrage in American history at the Pulse nightclub in Florida.

On average, twenty mass shootings occur every year in the United States; these devastating incidents usually last no more than twenty minutes and usually a lot less.

If you count the tally in war zones such as Afghanistan, Syria, Yemen, Libya, and Iraq, the number of incidents soars into the tens of thousands. Countless thousands of innocent people around the globe have been affected by situations of extreme danger played out in otherwise everyday settings—and there's no sign it will abate.

Indeed, new threats emerge with random knife and machete attacks in public places by jihadist beheaders intent on spreading raw terror.

This book represents a commonsense approach to the global epidemic of violent attacks on our society. People should hope for the best but be prepared for the worst in a world at war.

That's why I've drawn on my experiences to write this indispensable guide to the unacceptable realities of modern terror. My aim is to underpin your daily lives during these threatening times by giving you the knowledge to come out safely on the other side.

The title *Be a Hero* reflects the truth. You can be a hero simply by keeping your head while others panic. You can be a hero by offering emergency medical help at the scene.

You don't have to take on an active shooter to be a hero, but you are a hero if you do. Simply making a decision in the face of such danger is courageous. Being decisive is being heroic.

At the core of what I have to say lies an inalienable truth: We are not sheep. We do not have to wait to be slaughtered. We can act to protect ourselves.

Given good fortune, a brave heart, and the glimmer of an opportunity, the skills you learn in this book could help you stop an active shooter in his tracks.

God forbid you should ever need these skills. If you do, then I hope they'll help you to *Be a Hero*.

John Geddes
September 2016

Introduction

THE BIG PICTURE

Despite all the odds, the worst has happened and you've come under attack by bomb and bullet. The litany of fear will follow. Disorientation, hyperventilation, a heart-bursting pulse rate, surging adrenaline, and tunnel vision. You don't know which way to turn.

What do you do next? Who do you turn to? And which way should you turn? In the chapters that follow, this book will deal with all the issues in this broad-brush overview.

The aftermath of a bombing is an extreme environment, but I'll give you the knowledge to cope and the basic skills to help yourself and the injured.

An active shooter situation brings different challenges. I'll take you step-by-step through the decision-making processes that will enable you to evade and escape the killer.

I'll also talk you through some basic measures to help you to take direct action against an assailant if that's what you have to do. You may have no other choice. It may be a case of do or die.

The issues of a combined assault where an explosion is followed by a shooting attack will also be discussed. This is a particularly disorienting and confusing situation. I'll help you with it.

We'll take the three basic situations with which you may be confronted—a bombing, a shooting, or a combination of the two—and work through the permutations of the actions to take in each scenario.

Your response in the first few moments of an attack is vital and may ordain your personal outcome. The brain's emergency response system will flood your body with neurochemicals that prompt the primal responses of freeze, flight, or fight.

It was meant to be that way. Mankind first evolved to live and hunt among big, predatory beasts. The initial freeze response is designed to keep you from being spotted by a dangerous predator. That's precisely what an active shooter is—a dangerous predator.

Flight reflexes follow when your senses judge you have a chance of escape and your system is flooded with adrenaline. If the flight strategy is unsuccessful and you're unlucky enough to be cornered, the fight reflex kicks in. Make no mistake—in a life-threatening situation, you will find yourself fighting to the death.

Other chemical messages from the brain such as anger, revenge, or the desire to save the lives of others may trigger the fight reaction even if you have the option of escape.

Let's hope all those hardwired reflexes work. Let's hope you're so motionless you fade into the background and aren't noticed by an active shooter. Let's hope when you make a break for it, your timing is good enough not to catch a burst of automatic fire. If you decide to chance retaliating against the assailant, let's hope the fight reflex is so powerful that you take him down.

After the first seconds and minutes of relying on those Stone Age responses, you will then need to control and channel the effects of the adrenaline and cortisol chemicals surging through your system.

In effect, you've been turbocharged and you need to remove your foot from the pedal. Learn to regulate those urges and make more considered and rational choices to survive.

Knowledge leads to understanding, so in the chapters that follow, I'll explain the processes that unfold when the brain's danger radar sets off the chain reaction of freeze, flight, or fight. I'll explain how you can channel the surge of adrenaline into critical actions that will allow you to make the best of the worst possible situation.

These days, terror comes uninvited to our doorsteps. In the western democracies of Europe and the United States, jihadists deliberately target ordinary people going about their everyday business or during their leisure time. In the same way, paranoid gunmen run rampant through our communities and college campuses, killing indiscriminately.

The average profile of an active shooter is very consistent. In 98 percent of incidents the shooter acts alone. And 96 percent of them are men, which is why I will refer to them as "he" or "him" throughout the book.

Around 40 percent of events end when the active shooter commits suicide. Most of the remaining events end with him being shot. Very few shooters are taken alive.

Terrorist attacks are not confined to developed economies. Ordinary folk across Africa, the Middle East, and the Indian subcontinent are subjected to lethal sectarian attacks by bomb and bullet, too.

This book can help anyone, anywhere in the world. And to be clear, I have no intention of engaging in a rant about the evils of extreme Islam or in a critical commentary on the gun laws of any country.

Those issues are not my concern except where they dictate the way an attack is conducted. Motives are irrelevant when bullets are fired at random. Religious intolerance or voices in the head, jihadist or paranoid college nerd—it matters not. All that matters is survival.

Which brings me again to the title of this book—*Be a Hero*. It's fundamental. My definition of what constitutes a hero is not confined to the military heroics that win the Medal of Honor.

Society recognizes, and gratefully acknowledges, the gallantry of a trained soldier, sailor, or airman whose endeavors go above and beyond the call of duty. An unarmed, untrained civilian has some unique challenges to overcome yet is still able to exhibit heroism in different ways.

So, in my eyes, you're a hero if you survive a bombing or a shooting and then go on to give medical assistance to your wounded fellows. Similarly, if you manage to evade an active shooter and lead a group of terrified people to safety, then you're a hero. In the heat of the moment, some individuals might instinctively want to attack the assailant. This book offers you some core skills to be that hero, too. There are also documented cases of people taking a bullet to save the life of a loved one or, sometimes, a complete stranger. Such selfless valor is beyond words.

For the most part, police chiefs in the western world advise against direct action, promoting instead a "leave it to the experts" philosophy. I fundamentally disagree with them.

But I agree with the Homeland Security Department's advice: "As a last resort, attempt to take the active shooter down. When the shooter is at close range and you cannot flee, your chance of survival is much greater if you try to incapacitate him."

I'd go a step further and say there are situations when certain capable and determined individuals should actively seek confrontation with the shooter. This largely means people with combat experience and concealed carry–permit holders whose intervention could save innocent lives.

Often, long delays occur while official forces "clear" an area of active shooters. If you have a gut feeling that compels you to take action against a shooter, then do it. It may be a stark do-or-die choice. I'll help you with the task.

Male or female, heroes and heroines come in all shapes and sizes. Their qualities may be found in exciting acts of physical valor or far less obvious acts of courageous defiance.

I hope this book will help you to find the hero within. Whether you're a big strong warrior or a physically weaker individual, endowed with more than your share of courage, you will find out in the moment.

Whatever your personal qualities, it will help enormously if you realize one thing from the outset. Attacks with gun and bomb are executed without any consideration of mercy. Get this straight. Begging won't work; you will not be spared. Better to be prepared. You will have been thrown onto a roulette wheel. I want to help you beat the odds.

The first chapter of the book deals with fear. It contains some simple but effective techniques for recalibrating yourself and bringing the chemical urges generated by terror at least partially under control.

Let's assume you've spent a few moments doing that. Your heartbeat is slowing and you're breathing more regularly. What next? Well, you're in trouble and it's decision time.

The second chapter is about preparation. I will talk you through the techniques of Situational Awareness and Dynamic Risk Assessment.

Situational Awareness will give you a new way of looking at your surroundings and will make your daily life more vibrant. Dynamic Risk Assessment will provide you with a rolling, real-time analysis of your situation when danger strikes.

The third chapter recognizes that most of you will want to hide; most of you will want to flee the scene. That's a good strategy and I will go into detail about how best to escape and evade.

You'll learn the fascinating practicalities of cover from fire, skills that come as second nature to good soldiers navigating the dangerous terrain of a battlefield.

I'll explain the optimum places in which to take cover and which everyday objects and landmarks will afford the best protection. I'll also tell you where not to hide.

The fourth chapter will show you ways you can disrupt a shooter's tempo of killing and how to use everyday objects to turn the tables and create a zone of distraction and danger for him.

For those who find the resolve to fight back, the fifth chapter will talk you through vital strategies to help even the odds. I'll outline techniques for positioning yourself for an attack and show you how commonplace items can be used as weapons.

I'll also drill you in some highly effective Special Forces methods for disarming an active shooter. Attacking a shooter demands an uncompromising burst of savage violence on your part.

But remember, the law requires *you* to show restraint once the shooter has been disarmed and subdued. When he no longer presents an immediate danger, you are obliged to stop attacking him. Crazy as this may seem, desist from smashing him up any further. Otherwise, you might find yourself in trouble with the law or even sued by the shooter's family. Go figure.

The next chapter will tackle the growing problem of random knife and machete attacks, often aimed at beheading victims. These incidents are growing in number in Europe and have reared their heads here in the United States. I'll give you good strategies to foil a knife assault.

I can't emphasize enough that this is dangerous, last-ditch stuff. The decision can only be yours, and my advice may or may not save your life. But once decided, the knowledge you gain here will help you tackle terrorists with confidence and avoid targeted violence.

At this point, I want to underscore that there is very little in this book the bad guys can't access on jihadist or anarchist websites. After all, we live in an age where you can download instructions to make a dirty nuclear device with relative ease.

The bad guys spend their spare time studying and sharing this stuff online. I think it's time for good people to arm themselves with knowledge they would never, by inclination, use unless they had to in desperation.

The seventh chapter deals with those who are licensed to carry concealed handguns legally in certain jurisdictions. I'll outline strategies you can employ to use your weapon most effectively. I'll also point out some of the pitfalls of deploying your handgun and how to avoid them.

A concealed carry holder may kill the shooter with their weapon, but they'd do well to stop shooting when the assailant no longer has a weapon in hand. Essentially, you can kill him when he's armed but not when he's disarmed, although a thousand lawyers may have a thousand opinions on this.

The area where most people can make themselves useful is medical first response, which will be discussed in the eighth chapter. Be clear we're not talking about cuts and scrapes here. This is about traumatic battlefield injuries, crude amputations by explosion, and the catastrophic ripping and tearing of vital organs by shrapnel or bullets. It's uncompromising stuff, which demands the fainthearted should step up to the plate.

Paramedics will often be cordoned back until the area has been secured. I'll show you how to carry out a combat-style triage at the scene. Everyday materials can be used in the crucial task of controlling blood loss. I'll tell you how you how to do this.

In the ninth chapter, I'll deal with some of the issues surrounding the use of digital technology and social media by terrorists or their victims during the attacks themselves. It's a complex and difficult area. I'll advise you.

The chapters I've described so far concentrate on the theoretical aspects of surviving an active shooter event. My descriptions of the various possibilities of taking and breaking cover, making the environment hostile to the shooter and, in the final analysis, taking the shooter out are in the abstract.

Cynics among you might be forgiven for thinking: "No sir, that's just not possible. You'd get shot and killed within a heartbeat."

Well, believe me, all of it is possible. The last chapter will bring it all together and tie the theory in with reality. I'll describe well-documented and inspiring acts of heroism by everyday, ordinary people caught up in some of the country's and the world's most notorious active shooter events.

These clearly demonstrate that the lessons you will learn are based on fact. In that way, the abstract ideas will be brought to life.

I'll draw on case histories of active shootings like the Bataclan rock concert outrage in Paris, the Pulse nightclub shooting in Orlando, the Sandy Hook and Columbine school atrocities, and many others. The case histories contain accounts of inspiring individuals taking their fate into their own hands and turning the tables on terrorists.

This chapter is subdivided into categories such as schools, shopping malls, and movie theaters, allowing me to point out the different problems each environment presents and the best ways to tackle them.

We can learn from these tragedies. They totally back up the practical advice I'm offering. Many lives have been saved when individuals decide to "Be a Hero" in the midst of carnage.

Keep in mind this is not a step-by-step instruction manual. These chapters can't be followed in their sequence because each terror incident takes on a life of its own. The actions I outline may very well come up in a different sequence in a real terror event.

Recognize that all the strands must be drawn together to provide you with your best chance. Practice and learn the techniques I outline, then commit the combined knowledge from each chapter to your memory, and use them when it becomes relevant.

For instance, you may find yourself able to run for cover. The information from chapter three will guide you to find the best place.

When you get to relative safety, it's time to use the techniques outlined in chapter one to conquer your fear and mobilize the adrenaline rush to your advantage.

All the while, you will be accessing information you've learned from the other chapters to review your situation in a constantly changing assessment. It's what the military calls a rolling threat assessment. This skill, and the art of Situational Awareness, is covered in chapter two.

Natural leaders may emerge in your midst—maybe someone with military or police training. I'll help you to recognize and fall in constructively behind such a person. But it's my earnest belief this book will help you discover those very qualities of leadership within yourself.

Apply your judgment according to the mantra for those swept up in an active killer event. "Lead, follow, or get out of the way!" Gender is not relevant here. Male or female, it doesn't matter. All that matters is that someone steps up to the plate.

And when it counts, I believe what you read here will be in the back of your mind, ready to help you and others survive.

Along the way, I also hope to change your mind-set. Modern Western society has placed millions of us in a digital hall of mirrors. Reality is somewhere outside the social media bubble many of us exist in.

When people step out of their front doors, they take their social media bubble with them, insulating themselves from the world with earphones and constant texting.

It's your choice, but if I were you I'd leave the digital bubble at home. Forget your beats, and listen instead to the street sounds that will give the first indications of danger. Use your cell phone for strictly necessary communication, not for idle chatter.

I know a lot of people will reject this advice—which I detail in chapter nine—out of hand. But being involved with the world around you is a good call even outside the remit of this book. Be alive to the world and you'll be repaid with a new, vivid mind-set.

A terrorist event is not a video game, and computer algorithms won't help you when you're fighting for your life. There'll be no avatars on hand to assist. If and when it happens, you will have to look to yourself. You'll have to dig deep for real courage.

Clearly understand this, too. The purveyors of terror are not supermen. They are flesh and blood like you and me. Mostly, they're cowards finding courage in drugs and hiding behind the power of their weapons.

But they can be taken down, as history has shown. This book will give you the knowledge, the skills, and the resolve to meet their random violence with your own targeted counterattack. You can "Be a Hero," too, and never forget:

You are not a sheep and you don't have to wait in line to be slaughtered!

Chapter One

THE FEAR FACTOR

In this chapter I will explain the complex processes of the chemistry of fear. I will then outline simple ways of controlling fear. Understanding fear will help you control it. Controlling fear will help you survive.

We've all experienced something so frightening our senses were put into a spin. It might have been a near-miss collision on the highway or a strong current threatening a drowning.

Everyone experiences fear. Fear has a purpose. It is a survival mechanism; since the dawn of time our biology has been hard-wired with a "fight-or-flight" system. Not even Special Forces soldiers are immune from its heart-racing, gut-wrenching symptoms.

People in the military and first responders have learned, through endless drills, to channel their adrenaline rush into effective action. It's different for untried, untested civilians when they find themselves at the center of an essentially military situation—a suicide bombing or an active shooter attack.

No book can ever prevent you from experiencing fear if you are anywhere near a predatory active shooter. But I believe I can help you control your terror to the point where you'll be able to make a rational assessment of your situation and exercise judgment calls to best effect.

First, I'll describe the biology of fear in as simple terms as possible. Understanding what actually happens to your body takes you a long way down the road to bringing it under control. I am not a scientist but I've been assured what follows is an accurate description of the processes of fear, albeit in layman's terms.

The biology of fear

Your senses, most importantly sight and hearing, are constantly scanning the environment for signs of danger. When they detect a threat, the message is sent to the brain's command and control center, a walnut-shaped organ at the base of the brain called the amygdala.

This is an alarm-bell moment and the amygdala instantly fires off a chemical called glutamate, triggering two further command centers in the brain. The first goes under the name of the periaqueductal gray. This receptor orders the body to immediately jump out of the way or to freeze, depending on the information being fed from the senses. These reactions are reflex and completely automatic.

The other burst of the brain chemical glutamate shoots into the hypothalamus. It sparks our autonomic nervous system, kicking in the famous "flight-or-fight" reflex.

This network of hypothalamus, periaqueductal gray, and amygdala is known as the HPA axis. Once this is activated, the heart rate elevates and blood pressure rises. Adrenaline is pumped through the body, giving you the rush experienced when you feel fear. Blurred vision, perspiration, dry mouth, and a feeling of disconnect with reality may all follow.

The fear response has three characteristics, all designed as automatic survival mechanisms. The first is to freeze on the spot.

It evolved in the days of our earliest ancestors to prevent us from being noticed by dangerous predators such as lions or bears. In our scenario, the predator is an active shooter.

The second response is flight, which kicks in when your senses tell you there's no point staying put any longer. You've been spotted. The adrenaline already coursing through your cells that is looking for a release will be diverted to give you the superhero energy needed to run for your life.

The third response is the fight option, which kicks in when no options are left. So, when our senses say running away isn't possible, the adrenaline burst is redirected to fight off the threat by any and all means.

There's a stand-down switch too, a circuitry called the parasympathetic nervous system. It counters the fight-or-flight instinct by reversing the flood of adrenaline and lowering our heart rate back to normal.

The parasympathetic response is the reason why every time you have an unexpected scare, for instance a loud bang, the sudden surge of adrenaline is quickly reversed. The initial reaction is processed. The threat isn't real and the parasympathetic nervous system calms things down. Normal service resumes.

Many people suffer from the symptoms of imminent danger when there is no threat whatsoever. Those episodes are what we call panic attacks. They are not the same as authentic fear. They are serious medical conditions and they're not funny.

Medically, shock is a very different thing from fear and usually follows serious injury, including the effects of the blast wave generated by a bomb. A serious wound, from bomb or bullet, will induce a dramatic drop in blood pressure and can affect the major organs. This is a medical trauma that requires expert attention.

An odd fact is the direction of the blast wave from a bomb cannot be predicted. It's dictated by the physical surroundings at the explosion site. A solid desk might deflect the blast away and a person standing on the other side may survive unscratched and without any brain injury. It's the draw of a lottery.

For our purposes, we'll assume you have, by sheer good fortune, escaped a life-threatening injury and serious medical shock from a bomb.

Use the techniques I'm about to describe to calm down, after which you can put into play the battlefield medical techniques detailed in a later chapter.

You might survive a bombing only to find yourself in the midst of an active shooting attack, which immediately follows. If so, you can utilize the strategies laid out in the other chapters dealing with escape and evasion and, if necessary, attack.

When an active shooter comes into sight, you will either glue yourself to the spot or run for cover, depending on what your senses—your eyes and ears—tell you is required.

If you find safe cover but the active shooter is rapidly closing in on your location, the fight reflex may kick in. Indeed, you may be forced to take on the assailant for the slimmest chance of survival.

The chapters that follow will equip you with the knowledge you'll need to find cover and to take action. Once you've absorbed and practiced the information, it will stay in the back of your mind. We call it muscle memory. It becomes second nature. There's every reason to believe it will kick in if it's ever needed.

Calming techniques

You may find yourself in a hiding position for some time during an active shooter event. Use this period to bring the calming parasympathetic nervous system into play. There are a few techniques for doing this.

Reorient yourself

The first thing to do is to bring yourself back to the moment. Time will have taken on a dreamlike quality. Events will seem to be unfolding in slow motion. You will be experiencing a feeling of unreality. *What's going on? Is this really happening to me?*

Begin by carefully checking yourself over. Do this by subjecting your body to the maximum possible examination. Rub your hands over your torso, your legs, and your arms.

As you check yourself, look at your hands constantly for signs of blood or other fluids indicating an injury. Gently feel your head and face. Touch and look slowly and methodically. Don't forget your armpits.

There's been shooting. Has any flying debris struck you? Check yourself for signs of trauma. Have you sprained an ankle or hurt a shoulder when diving for cover? Put your limbs through their normal range of movement and check for pain and symmetry.

This is all information you need to know before you decide on either flight or fight. It's also important you make a mental note of any injuries to pass on to the medical professionals when they arrive. But it also represents a vital technique to bring you back to a sense of reality. It pulls your mind back into your body.

Next, look at your watch. Make a mental note of the time. Count up to thirty seconds. Again, this will bring your mind back to the immediate moment. It's known that counting can help take the HPA axis offline and allow your nervous system to reboot. It can be particularly effective if you've had a knock to your head.

Similarly, taking an inventory of textures and colors can help. Remind yourself that you are wearing a blue suit and black shoes. Experts call these techniques Sensory Input, and they help to bring the prefrontal cortex, the decision-making part of the brain, back into play.

Once you've done this, you can start to make observations of the scene you find yourself in. The military calls this a Dynamic Risk Assessment. It is a vital forerunner to making life-or-death decisions. I will discuss Dynamic Risk Assessment in the following chapter of the book.

If these simple techniques haven't worked and you are still in a high state of fear, indecision, and confusion, there are some very effective breathing exercises you can try.

Breathing exercises

I recommend you practice all these techniques until they're second nature. They'll also prove useful in dealing with everyday, personally traumatic situations such as accidents or even bereavement.

These breathing exercises will help you self-regulate and calm yourself in the midst of the trauma. The first is Paced Breathing, and it's a quick way to bring your fear at least partially under control.

Two techniques are involved in Paced Breathing. In the first, you count slowly for sixty breaths while focusing your attention on the out breaths, the exhalations. Breathe in. Breathe out, then count.

Alternatively, you can try another version of Paced Breathing called diaphragmatic breathing. This time you will breathe in for a count of four and breathe out for a count of eight. Repeat this for ten breaths and focus on the exhalation each time.

Both techniques are good ways of stimulating your parasympathetic system to kick into action. This, in turn, lets your mind clear itself and lucid thought processes to reengage. You should be able to assess far more clearly what to do next. In an active shooter situation, clarity of decision is absolutely vital.

So far so good, but there are also a couple of other help-ful breathing strategies. One of them is called Inter-Palmal Self-Regulation and it goes like this.

Place one hand on your forehead and the other hand on your chest. Breathe in and out three times, focusing on the exhalation. Move your hand from the forehead to the belly. Inhale and exhale three times again.

Employing these strategies in the midst of trauma and chaos may seem challenging because while you are trying to calm your-self, your nervous system is insisting on maintaining a state of fight-or-flight.

However, these exercises will help you recalibrate the nervous system from a state of hyperarousal. You begin to think clearly again and make reasoned judgments so vital in your situation. Try them all and see which one may suit you best and, most impor-tantly, the one you can best commit to memory.

Scenarios

I'll recap here for the different scenarios, assuming you have not been badly injured:

A Bombing

Check yourself over. Trace your hands slowly and deliberately over your limbs and torso, checking for any damage, however minor, to your body. Check your head and face in the same way.

Go immediately into the calm-down drills. Look at your watch and count the second hand to thirty. Begin the Paced Breathing exercises you have already practiced and committed to memory.

Either:

Count slowly for sixty breaths while focusing on the exhalations. Count them off when you breathe out.

Or:

Breathe in for a count of four and breathe out for a count of eight. Repeat this for ten breaths. Again focus on the exhalation.

You should now be in a less heightened state of fear, so start looking for people to help. How you can help will be explained in chapter five, which deals with battlefield first response.

An Active Shooter

The first few seconds will be dictated by the actions of the shooter and by your reflexes. You will freeze or you will dive for cover.

If your reactions have succeeded in taking you to relative safety, begin the same calming drills as indicated above.

When you have brought yourself back to time and place, follow the instructions in the rest of the book for escape and evasion, attacking an active shooter, and first medical response.

A Bombing Followed by an Active Shooting

You'll have no choice but to go with your instincts for the first few seconds. People will already have been killed by the bomb. People will no doubt be killed by the shooter.

If you survive the bombing and the first seconds of the shooting, take cover and go through your drills.

Decompress. Assess. Decide.

There's one more strategy to bring the fear factor under control once you've reestablished yourself in time and place. Think of those you love and begin to repeat this basic truth:

"I'm not a sheep. I won't wait to be slaughtered."

Chapter Two

WHAT IF?

This chapter will explain two key skills you should develop in your everyday life. The first is Situational Awareness, or, to put it very simply, gaining insights by watching what goes on around you.

The second skill is Dynamic Risk Assessment, the ability to weigh up the risks of a crisis situation as it rapidly unfolds. The results of that assessment will reward you with your options and, crucially, dictate your next move.

Like other combat arena professionals, I have been ingrained with the skill of Situational Awareness through training and necessity. It now comes as second nature. On the occasions I consciously think about awareness, I find it reassuring to know I have a basic handle on my surroundings. It's time for you to learn about these crucial skills.

Situational Awareness

In everyday language, Situational Awareness is the ability to know what's going on around you. It's the combination of observation and insight. You'll learn the skills of an experienced tracker, but you'll apply them in the modern urban environment, not the back-woods wilderness.

This skill comes on two levels. The first is learning to observe what's happening at any given moment, a general awareness of your surroundings.

The second is using your observations to adapt your behavior. Identifying subtle changes in your environment allows you to regulate your internal threat alert.

The objective is to create a new mind-set allowing you to be aware, yet relaxed, as you move through your daily life. This is not a daunting prospect but a reassuring one.

Situational Awareness will give you a head start in the event of a terror attack. This awareness of your surroundings will also enhance your life in unexpected ways. You'll find these insights into your environment will add vibrancy to your everyday existence.

There's no surprise in this. Our hunter-gatherer ancestors lived life with a heightened sense of being, simply to survive in the hostile environment they moved through. They noticed change and were primed to deal with danger. They had to.

The same applies today; only the nature of those threats has changed. Our ancestors were on the alert for big predators such as bears and lions. Today, we're on the lookout for robbers and terrorists.

Let's look more closely at observation first. You may have heard the military term "your Six." It comes from the World War II airmen who described the sky around them in the terms of a tactical clock, with twelve o'clock the space directly in front of them. Six, then, is directly behind and, of course, out of sight.

Watching your Six means watching your back. This concept leads many combat zone specialists to instinctively look for a seat with a back to the wall. Out of habit they usually choose a spot with a view of the door when in a bar or restaurant.

The ability to view the comings and goings and to assess the general demeanor of people is reassuring and paradoxically allows you to relax. You will have established a viewing platform that allows you to chill while never entirely dropping your guard.

There's another vitally important line of sight rule on the tactical clock. It's a vital principle, which you can employ in your favor against an active shooter. It's called the Ten to Two and it is described below.

Human beings are predators by evolution. That means we have two features in common with most other predators: canine teeth and forward-facing eyes.

Forward-facing eyes are designed to focus intensely on prey fleeing ahead of us. Hence, most prey animals have eyes that see around a large part of the "clock" of their eyesight. This type of vision helps give them early warning of predators. We do not have that facility. We only see sharply from our Ten to our Two.

Taking the shooter's Twelve as his view directly in front, do your level best to keep to either side of his Ten or his Two.

Outside his Ten and Two, his vision fades from peripheral to zero sight. Peripheral sight has minimal detection of movement and color. To focus on what is essentially a blur to him, the shooter will have to turn his head. Firing at the new target requires him to realign his body, or swing the gun unsighted to fire at the blur. Either way, he is a microsecond slower or a foot or two less accurate.

The predatory shooter thrives on the narrow sight band around his Twelve and out to his Ten to Two. This is where he observes and targets the frozen or fleeing herd of humans.

It's vital you keep out of his Ten to Two at all times. As a rule, stay low and move fast out of the Ten to Two zone. This is a continual, real-time, rolling priority for you.

The Ten to Two rule is a key to escape and evasion. You will learn later it's also a key rule when it comes to attacking the shooter.

Be aware of the Ten to Two rule. It could save you.

I am not for a moment suggesting going through life like a Secret Service agent body-guarding the president. There's no need to go through life swiveling your head like a gun turret locating potential targets. Peering through sunglasses at passersby as though they were a potential threat doesn't help one bit.

The state of mind you are looking to develop is one of relaxed vigilance. It allows you to go about your life in an easygoing way but always to be one step ahead of the herd because you're able to spot a threat developing.

You don't need to shred your own nerves by constant overstimulation. Hypervigilance is counterproductive. It fogs your mind and tricks you into seeing so many perceived threats you'll miss the one you need to notice: the real one.

Get to know your surroundings. You'd be very foolish to go for a mountain hike without knowing alternative trails to bring you safely down at the end of the day.

Familiarize yourself with your local shopping mall, the main street you visit most often, favorite bars and restaurants, movie theaters you patronize.

You may think you know these places well, but I guarantee if a crisis occurred you would find your knowledge of emergency exits and alternative routes sadly lacking. Look at these locations again, but this time, do so with an analytical eye.

Familiarize yourself with all the exits, all the side streets and alleys. Look at these places through different eyes. Make a note of emergency exits and where they take you. Look for doors in stores and restaurants that lead out to loading bays. Note where there are janitors' cupboards or kitchens leading to outside service doors.

There are important reasons for taking particular note of and familiarizing yourself with the location of janitors' storerooms and restaurant kitchens. I will explain these reasons in chapter four.

It's important you realize there are two dimensions to the urban landscape: the public forum and the workers' service infrastructure. Understanding that interface between the public and the off-limits areas may be the key to surviving an incident.

That's why, if the time should come, you needn't worry about moving quickly through the "Staff Only" door in a store to find the rear loading area. If an active shooter event starts, you must not be shy about accessing these off-limits areas for reasons of escape and evasion. Why would you be?

You can practice these skills in a fun way on your home turf and even involve partners and children. You don't have to tell kids there is a serious intent behind the game, but it will help them develop good observational skills, which in any event will enhance their lives.

Before you visit your main street or the local mall, tell them you're going to play a new version of I Spy with My Little Eye. In this version you set the challenge by asking them to memorize all the emergency exits, security staff, fire extinguishers, etc. they can spot.

At the end of the visit you quiz them. You get the picture. You're having some fun, the kids are enjoying a challenge, and you're developing knowledge and observational skills. You're teaching them to be mindful of their environment. That's a great life-enhancing skill.

When you're away from your usual haunts in your neighborhood, try to make a rapid reconnaissance of any new environment you find yourself in. Get used to scanning all new streetscapes for alternative escape routes.

Military personnel, law enforcement officers, and experienced media correspondents are among those professionals who do a running internal assessment of their surroundings instinctively and unconsciously. So do criminals and terrorists. Get used to doing the same.

It's vital to develop your Situational Awareness skills by looking critically at the locations you visit that are not familiar. When you visit new locations, use the same "eyes on" approach to quickly assimilate as much information as you can.

This enhanced observational skill will allow you to make considered decisions in time of attack—and it allows you to make them very quickly. Observations will give you the edge. In time, like a war zone veteran, it will become second nature and I know you'll feel good about it.

So you've developed observational skills including lay-of-the-land knowledge and basic checking-your-Six skills. But there's more, and you must learn to adapt and to watch for telltale signs of looming danger.

Adapt in this context means configuring the knowledge you've gained from your observations to create a norm. That's the baseline where everything is in order. All is normal.

Wherever you are, you have a standard model of normality in your mind. When an inconsistency or irregularity shows up—something suspicious or out of the ordinary—you must be ready to respond to that.

Of course, what constitutes "normal" differs from environment to environment. The normal standard in the Pulse nightclub in Orlando was a cacophony of loud music, shrieks, and laughter. The baseline of behavior in the *Charlie Hebdo* magazine office in Paris was a relatively quiet, businesslike atmosphere.

Observe and lay down what you believe to be the normal baseline in any environment and then be ready to adapt and respond if it changes.

This requires you to have a plan in mind, a strategy that will render you and yours safe. Combine this with the advice on Dynamic Risk Assessment you'll find in the second part of this chapter and you'll be equipped to make a superfast "on the run" strategy.

In military terms the telltale signs of impending trouble are called Combat Indicators. They include the demeanor and behavior of people in your vicinity. It is not beyond the realm of possibility that you may find yourself close to someone who is about to initiate an active shooting event. Recognition could lead to prevention.

Raise your internal threat alert levels to match your suspicion and that may prompt you to act against a threat either by removing yourself and loved ones from the area or by directly challenging a suspect.

For your purposes, the most important telltale behavioral signs that diverge from the norm will be in body language. All of us, including terrorists, have conscious and subconscious tics of body language.

General traits of behavior can be observed. When a person sets out with an aggressive action in mind, their body chemistry changes their posture whether they like it or not.

Smoldering adrenaline may result in a perpetrator unwittingly engaging in postures and gestures that are designed, by his body chemistry, to make him feel bigger, more intimidating, and dominant.

Such behavior is likely to attract your attention. You will observe it. You will then adapt your threat perception and begin planning for a response to any aggression that may manifest itself.

Similarly, a person who looks agitated, fidgety, and nervous may come to your attention. He or she may simply be nervous on their way to a dental appointment. Or they may be carrying a weapon. Observe their behavior. Factor it in, adapt your threat assessment, and be ready to respond to any ramping up of this unusual behavior.

Often, people bound on a criminal mission will be doing the same as what I am recommending you do. They'll be scanning their surroundings and they'll have chosen a back-to-the-wall, observational position in a room or streetscape. They'll be checking their own Six.

Observe that behavior, adapt your threat level assessment, and be prepared for further irregularities or anomalies that will prompt you to act.

The obverse of this situation is someone visibly too relaxed when everyone else is completely tense. If an individual seems unperturbed by an explosion in the vicinity when everyone else is alarmed, he could be an accomplice.

He may not be alarmed because he was expecting the explosion. Factor that in and, obviously in this situation, act immediately. Take him down just in case. You can always sort it out later. In fact, this trait allowed police to quickly identify the Boston bombers from pictures of the crowd at the time. They didn't look at all surprised.

The first Combat Indicators I learned about in Special Forces terrorist training had to do with the hands. It's well known in military and law enforcement circles that hands can be a complete giveaway.

If someone is constantly checking and rechecking a part of their body by patting it or feeling it through their clothing, they may have something to hide. Perhaps it's completely innocent and they're just checking that they've still got an envelope with a winning lottery ticket.

Or maybe they've got something sinister to hide. A drug stash, perhaps. Or, for our purposes, a concealed weapon. Again, consider the possibilities. Adapt, and keep a sharp eye on this person. It could save lives.

When an active shooter event happens, you'll be in a situation where your brain will be forced to process a great deal of information in microseconds.

In this next part of the chapter, I'll help you cope with this potential overload of data. The process of evaluating all this information, sifting through it for what is relevant to survival, is known as Dynamic Risk Assessment.

Dynamic Risk Assessment

The generally agreed definition of a Dynamic Risk Assessment is "the continuous process of identifying hazards, assessing risk, taking action to eliminate or reduce risk, monitoring and reviewing risk, in the rapidly changing circumstances of an incident."

In simple terms, we all carry out Dynamic Risk Assessments subconsciously to protect ourselves on a daily basis. It's a basic instinct you all are familiar with.

On a day-to-day level, one obvious example of Dynamic Risk Assessment is stepping off a sidewalk to cross the street. You look both ways to check for oncoming vehicles before crossing the street—that's if you want to survive the simple task.

What you have done is carry out a risk assessment. You were probably taught to make that simple safety check when you were a child.

You get the idea. Now multiply that into a whole list of situations, from climbing a ladder to swimming in a river. The height of a building and the availability of a safe place to lean your ladder are considered and assessed before you commit.

The width of that river, the depth, and how clear the water is will be processed. And before you take the plunge, you'll be looking for signs of how fast the current is running—for example, the speed of a branch swept downstream.

There are countless factors to be considered before committing to a risky situation. Naturally, these factors vary from situation to situation and from threat to threat and, on a day-to-day level, you'll have time to consider your assessment and come to a decision about it.

The process becomes dynamic or kinetic when events accelerate and unfold in seconds and microseconds. For instance, when your ladder becomes unstable or you are caught up in a river current.

Your senses will be continually assessing and reassessing your situation. Your sight and hearing, in particular, will feed your brain with the information it needs for you to make a rational and successful decision.

That decision may stabilize your situation and keep you out of harm's way. In other words, you will have gone into survival mode. This is precisely what happens when you're enmeshed in an active shooter event.

But this time the danger has been thrust upon you. You have no choice in the matter. On top of that, the time factor of your assessment is critically compressed. You've been swept away on the current of a highly violent event and it is all too easy to make the wrong move.

However, it is still entirely possible to make sense out of the confusion. It is still possible to make some basic and ultrarapid evaluations of your situation.

Remember that active shooter incidents are essentially combat situations, and in the military world the skills of a Dynamic Risk Assessment are described in different terms. They are written tactical instructions known here in the United States as Combat Estimates. In Canada and the United Kingdom they're called Battlefield Appreciation.

The idea is to ask yourself a set of standard questions that have been carefully calculated and laid out by combat experts in the Pentagon and are designed for use in the heat of battle.

They are tried-and-tested, rule-of-thumb checklists that soldiers are trained to use when they are engaged in a rapidly evolving combat. You can use something very similar.

In essence, this checklist enables a soldier to slow things down in his or her mind and to rationally evaluate a situation, enabling the soldier to decide on the least risky and most likely successful course of action.

Some of the items on the military checklist are classified. However, there are a few I've distilled into simple language for the benefit of readers who are not familiar with military jargon.

A soldier will run through the important elements in the risk equation. He or she will consider the nature of the fighting ground, the number and disposition of the enemy, and the number and position of any friendly forces.

You can translate those into what's going on in your vicinity, whether that's a shopping mall, a major transport hub, a city street, an office block, or a nightclub.

How many shooters are there? Are you able to identify their locations? Are there any police or other friendly forces on hand? If not, are there any individuals who will join you in a unit?

Having gone through this list, you can then pose yourself a couple of important questions: Who and why?

They're important because the answers have a huge bearing on your survival. You then apply the last vital question to what you've deduced and processed so far. It's the key question: *What If?*

If you conclude the active shooters are robbers in the course of a heist, then you might reasonably conclude they won't shoot at you unless you attempt to intervene. Your best plan would be to escape the scene.

What if you recognize that you've been caught up in a terror event and you have identified an active shooter intent on killing as many people as possible?

Go through the various sequences and scenarios I've outlined. Calm yourself with the techniques described in chapter one. Just as in the case of a robbery, you will seek the best route out. But in this case another "What if" will guide you.

What if the terrorists have set a trap at escape exits? Pay great attention to this possibility and your escape attempt will be more cautious, more tactical.

This means you must not become one of the herd. Pace your escape so you are paying as much attention to what is going on in front of you as you are to the danger pursuing you behind.

If escape is not possible then use the information you'll find in the next chapter to find safe cover. Then try to organize like-minded individuals to hamper the activities of the assailant and possibly attack the shooter.

This strategy will be outlined in chapters four and five. These describe reasonably simple methods for obstructing the progress of an active shooter and, in the final analysis, attacking him.

Be fully aware that active shooters and bombers also make their own risk assessments. However, in their upside-down world it is a negative assessment as, in most cases, they've already factored their own deaths into the equation.

The risks they are concerned with are the risks associated with not being able to kill a sufficient number of people. They will be assessing whether they can stay alive long enough to expend all their ammunition on their victims. The risk they most fear is the risk of being thwarted in their aim of maximum carnage.

Knowing this will help you when you make a critical assessment of your situation. It will help you in deciding "What if" you attempt to hamper an active shooter's rampage. I'll explain exactly why and how you can do this in chapter four.

So, if you have followed my advice, you'll already be scanning your environment for alternative routes to take you, and anyone with you, out of danger.

That approach will also help you to focus mentally if you become trapped in a terror event. As well as providing you with a tactical platform to work on, it will prove as useful as the self-calming exercises outlined in chapter one.

I know this to be a fact because when the shooting starts in a war zone, a great many military personnel find the process of making a Combat Estimate a calming factor.

Mind and body respond to the process of going through all the salient facts of your situation and the available options. This systematic approach of assessing all the information puts you firmly back in time and place.

Remember, observation and risk assessment in real time can make all the difference. Observing and adapting to a rolling risk assessment means you are taking destiny into your own hands.

* * *

To recap the advice in this chapter:

Situational Awareness is simply knowing what's going on around you—being present in your environment.

To do that successfully, you should have a good handle on the environment you are in. So get to know your regular haunts in some detail.

Apply the same analytical eye to new places you're visiting. You will find it surprising how Situational Awareness enhances life in general.

Check your Six. Settle in locations with a good all-round view.

Learn the Ten to Two rule

Body Language. Look out for the telltale signs of individuals who potentially have violent intent.

Be aware. Be ready to act.

Dynamic Risk Assessment is a rolling, real-time appraisal of your situation. It requires a mind-set that harnesses your mental awareness to your physical actions.

Who, what, where, when, and why? These are the Dynamic Risk Assessment questions you must constantly assess and reassess.

Constantly run the answers you come up with against the big question: **What if?**

What if? Allows you to make a rational decision in a fluidly moving situation based on the balance of probabilities.

Chapter Three

THE QUESTION OF COVER

This chapter deals with the important subject of taking and breaking cover in an active shooter event. This includes the issue of escape for people with disabilities, the elderly, and infants. It also offers advice on crisis leadership and communicating with the authorities.

Statistically, you will most likely be in a busy, crowded location when an active shooter strikes. It could be a shopping mall, a movie theater, a transport hub like an airport, or an office. It can be any place where people are drawn together in large numbers.

These locations are known, in the official jargon, as PMGs— "Places of Mass Gathering." They have another designation—one that graphically explains why Places of Mass Gathering are the natural target of choice for a terrorist. They are also known as "Target-Rich Environments."

With few exceptions, Places of Mass Gathering in the developed world should have a crisis management strategy put in place to deal with any emergency. Whether it's a major fire, an earthquake, or a terrorist attack, those in charge need a plan. In the case of terror attacks, all government departments and educational establishments will have been risk-assessed by professionals, and a strategy will have been carefully drawn.

Key management personnel and staff will have been trained in various roles including lockdown procedures and evacuation policies. In most cases, the owners of commercial locations will have paid security consultants to go through the same process and draw up a rational and well-thought-out emergency routine called a Lockdown Plan.

Have little faith that these well-laid formulas work out because almost all that is rational is thrown to the wind when a bomb explodes or an active shooter strikes. Hopefully, you will have taken in and practiced the techniques of Situational Awareness as outlined in the previous chapter.

If so, you may have anticipated a terror event brewing and already be moving toward safety. You will instinctively use the knowledge of your environment as you go about your daily routine. Those I Spy games with the kids can pay dividends.

The techniques of fear control I discussed in chapter one will help you stay calm and focused. The mind strategies of Dynamic Risk Assessment, outlined in the last chapter, will also be coming into play. They will help you get through a passage of time that seems to be moving in slow motion but is, in fact, unfolding at a breakneck pace.

All these techniques will be needed to navigate your way through a phenomenon described in one of the most overworked clichés I know. That phenomenon is called "the fog of war."

The term originated from the blanket of smoke generated by black powder on the battlefield. And while it may be overused, I've never heard a better way of describing the chaos that ensues in the wake of armed violence.

Most active shooter events last fifteen minutes at most, around eight on average, but the chaos lasts much longer with an aftermath of wounded people in need of urgent medical help.

Expect to look after yourself without any practical assistance from the authorities for a relatively long time. It varies with different jurisdictions, but the law enforcement authorities will often not allow paramedic assistance into an area until they have declared it free of active shooters.

Everything depends on the attitude, skill, and operational directives of the assaulting unit involved in its attempts to rescue you. But do not count on any medical help for up to an hour—and sometimes a lot longer. You will have to fend for yourself.

In chapter eight, I'll tell you how you can deploy battlefield medic techniques to help the wounded until help eventually arrives. This is an important chapter. First-response medical assistance to the wounded is how most people can render the most help to the greatest number of victims.

Some jihadist events, typically involving more than one active shooter, develop into much longer pitched battles once the forces of law and order arrive on the scene. This has happened, notably in hotel complexes or malls, because the terrorists engage in partial hostage-taking to provide themselves with human shields. This is done to deliberately extend the length of the terror event.

I use the term "partial hostage-taking" because there is no serious intention to use those taken as pawns in prolonged negotiations. Their status is starkly that of murder victims in waiting. The moment the hostage becomes a tactical burden, or when the active shooter believes he is about to be neutralized, the hostage is executed.

Priority one is to avoid contact with the killers. The obvious solution to this is to find a route out of the location and away from danger.

Priority two is to bring some order to the chaos and rally at least a few of those who are fleeing from the shooter into a make-shift self-defense unit.

I will discuss those priorities soon, but first I want to remind you of the massive benefits of Situational Awareness if the worst happens and you're caught up in a terror event.

Using your observational skills

There's a famous old military dictum: "Time Spent in Reconnaissance is Seldom Wasted." It's good advice, so take it and familiarize yourself with the Places of Mass Gathering you regularly use.

Take my advice and have a fresh look at your favorite shopping malls, the transport hubs you use for your commute, the hotels, movie theaters, and bars you frequent.

I went through much of this in the previous chapter, but believe me, I am not repeating this advice for the sake of it. I am reinforcing these points because they are vitally important.

Understand that the interface between public spaces and the business infrastructure of a location may be the key to surviving an incident. I hope you'll take note of emergency exit locations and where they'll lead you.

Look for doors that lead to loading bays. Note where janitors' closets or kitchens lead to outside service doors. They may provide you with a safe escape route. They may also give you a great resource in the event you are forced to take further measures to protect yourself and your loved ones.

When an active shooter event begins, immediately look for an escape route and keep moving away from the shooting. Consciously acquire anything you can lay your hands on to use as a weapon or to obstruct active shooters. I will go into detail about the things you should be looking for and how you can use them in chapter four.

Remember the Ten to Two rule. Keep out of the line of fire.

Call emergency services as soon as possible and give them a running commentary of events as they unfold. But whatever you do, keep moving away from the threat.

Finding a route to safety may not be as simple as it sounds. The problem is that you won't be the only one who has thought of this; everyone else will be rushing to the exits.

The obvious escape routes will become crowded with frightened, panicking people very quickly. By using his weapon, the active shooter is making himself top of the predator chain in the area. He wants to stampede the rest of us because that gives him a lot of victims to pick off at will.

We evolved as predators, not as herd animals. With our forward-facing eyes, herding together while in panic is a particularly disturbing situation for humans. We are not designed for stampedes. Avoid becoming one of the herd.

You can try to influence at least part of the stampede near you into taking a different, more positive course of action. You might be able to turn a frightened group into a unit. You might turn some of the herd into a pack.

Lead, Follow, or Get Out of the Way

After reading this book, you may feel you have sufficient knowledge and confidence to lead people and to optimize their chances of survival. If you believe you have what it takes, call out orders clearly and loudly to those around you.

If you are a veteran or a serving soldier with combat experience, call that information out. It may seem obvious, but not many soldiers find themselves entangled with civilians in harm's way. So call it out and gather people to you. It may also reassure them.

When you've decided to take on a leadership role, a good first move is to help people stop panicking by delivering your own Dynamic Risk Assessment of the situation as you have formulated it.

This, of course, will depend on the circumstances around you. While you are speaking, use your hands to clearly signal the directions of danger and escape to those you are addressing.

It may go something like the following:

"There's one shooter. He's in that direction [pointing]. He's coming our way. There's a door this way [clearly pointing] that leads to the parking lot."

If you are certain of a route that is not obvious, simply shout: "Follow me!"

There may be frightened children present, so you might clearly order someone: "Bring the children this way!"

There will be many variations on this sort of command depending on the unfolding circumstances. Remember, you are giving orders and if you deliver them with authority, people will react positively. They'll be attracted to you like iron filings to a magnet.

Those who respond are those with the will to change the outcome of a seemingly one-sided and disastrous situation. You all will have behaved admirably, regardless of your fate.

Similarly, you may decide that someone else, maybe a vet with combat experience, is the one to follow. Do it, and remember the important principle: Lead, Follow, or Get Out of the Way.

Other characters may present themselves. There may be a loudmouth or a know-it-all among the people in the trapped herd. We've all met them in our communities and workplaces.

If you feel someone of this description is misleading people through ignorance, don't waste time arguing with them. Move on. Follow your instincts and use the knowledge you've gathered from this book.

Remember, the scenario will unfold in seconds and micro-seconds. The sound of approaching gunfire. Questioning voices. Confusion. Screams. Hints of movement in your peripheral vision. All these combine to give time a surreal quality during an incident.

A small percentage of people have an almost magical way of dealing with time. These include great sportsmen and sportswomen and a lot of very good soldiers. Be aware that what you believe is unfolding slowly is really happening in a dynamic time frame.

At certain points in the unfolding attack, you may need to stay quiet so as not to attract an active shooter's attention. Practice these hand signals with your loved ones so you can communicate with them during an emergency:

Indicate the number of shooters by holding fingers up. It may be one, two, or three for instance.

To indicate the direction in which the active shooter or shooters are operating, make a thumbs-down sign, then point in that direction with an open palmed hand, fingers closed together.

If you want an individual to come to your place of cover for their own safety, put one hand on your head. It means *come to me*.

If you want them to come to you urgently, pump your closed fist up and down which means *come to me quickly/run!*

Finger to your lips means *Silence!*

Open palm to your ear *Listen!*

Looking in a particular direction with your hand across your face, fingers open, means that an ambush or attack is imminent in that direction. Take cover and prepare to attack.

These hand signals can be indispensable in the event of an incident, so practice them. Hopefully, your loved ones will never need them, but make sure they understand those signals in case they do.

Do not believe that once you have reached the emergency exit of a building you are in the clear. There may be more than one active shooter and they will certainly have scoped out the target prior to their attack.

This happened in the Bataclan nightclub attack in Paris. An active shooter was waiting in the lane outside the emergency exit from the club. As a stampede of people ran to "safety," the shooter claimed many victims as they poured through the exit.

The security forces can also be unpredictable. A police counter-attack in Australia at a siege ended when the gunman shot himself. The security forces present were confused and killed two hostages in the panic that ensued. This also occurred in Paris.

Do not congregate with others in open spaces. Avoid the evacuation points designated by authorities "in case of fire" unless told to do so by security forces.

These areas could well become killing fields. Look for alternative exits, emergency doors, windows, or trade entrances. When you have escaped, make sure you turn back any civilians heading toward the killing zone who may be unaware of what has happened.

If you are not already trapped with them, I would not voluntarily join the herd. Instead, I'd act counterintuitively and head away from the panicked crowd and the shooter.

I would look for a less obvious and less crowded route out of the line of fire. If I couldn't find one, then I would look for cover. Taking cover is the fallback position if you are convinced, by your rolling assessment, that fleeing the scene is no longer an option.

Types of cover

There are basically two types of cover: soft cover and hard cover. Some people call them concealment and cover.

Soft cover or concealment is an object or feature that hides you from sight but does not have sufficient strength to protect you from bullets. A long drape in a window could provide concealment but it's never going to protect you. It's really not ideal but remember: out of sight, out of mind.

Hard cover hides you from sight but is of sufficiently strong material to afford you protection from bullets.

At this point, I'll explain the concept of "dead ground" to help you better understand the idea of cover. This concept is familiar to combat infantrymen who live or die by the use of dead ground when under fire.

Dead ground is all about angles. Let me give you an example. During one intense firefight I spent hours under heavy machine-gun fire while in relative safety. I could even move along routes hidden from the line of sight of direct fire.

Lethal .50 caliber rounds were zipping a few inches above my head while I ate my field rations. Dozens of my comrades were in the same situation and lived to tell the tale.

We were able to survive in this extremely hostile environment because we'd found cover in dead ground. The enemy machine-gun crews were simply not able to elevate or decline their barrels to an angle that could kill us. If they moved from their carefully entrenched positions to do so, we could have killed them.

You can use the concept of dead ground to great effect in an active shooter situation. Use the architectural furniture of your location to your advantage. A brick wall, a staircase, a curbstone, or a steel joist can give you cover with the advantage of dead ground out of the arc of fire.

You will be able to frustrate the shooter with angles he can't overcome without wasting time in moving. Why go out of his way to shoot you when he can find multiple, easier targets closer at hand with no cover?

Intelligent use of cover makes you a difficult target. You will not be worth the effort to a shooter, intent on maximizing his kills, when there are easier targets around.

Never break cover from the same place as you took cover. This may allow an active shooter to second-guess you. You'll be making a predictable move.

Many advisory notes issued by official government sources recommend finding a room, then locking and barricading yourself inside for cover. They say move away from the door, stay silent, and silence your mobile phone. Remain there until rescuers advise you to move, or if you are forced to move because of imminent threat from an active shooter.

I don't necessarily agree with this strategy. I wouldn't recommend staying in a room with only one entrance or exit unless it's a last resort or you are already trapped.

Once inside, you have no choice but to wait until you're rescued or until the killer finds you. However, if you find yourself in this situation, there are ways of protecting yourself, which I will go into in chapter four.

Constantly look for fresh cover: walls, stairways, pillars. Brick or steel provides the best hard cover. Wood is not generally good protection. If it's a thin sheet, it will barely slow down a round. However, multiple layers of wood, support beams, and heavy-duty wooden architectural features will deflect bullets.

Move from cover to cover. Utilize the dead-ground effect. Stay low and move as fast as you are able.

Stay low! Move fast! Keep out of a shooter's Ten to Two!

If you find a room to hide in, first check it through the open door. See if it has another way out, be it a door or a window. If you are high up in a building, a window to the outside will be of little use.

Check if the door can be locked from the inside, and see if it's thick and sturdy. Glance inside for furniture that might provide good barricade material. In an office or a classroom, a filing cabinet will make great cover only if it's full of paper files. If it's empty, rounds will go straight through it.

If you feel the room meets all these requirements, then you may judge it to be a safe haven. If not, move on quickly. Make a rapid decision. Nothing is to be gained from an internal debate about the qualities of a room. If you are not certain after one examination just move on.

Remember: Stay low. Move fast

If the incident is in the street, then parked vehicles may be used as cover. However, forget about the movies. Do not think the thin metal skin of a standard car will keep you safe. High-velocity rounds will go through soft-skinned civilian vehicles like butter— in one side and out the other.

A vehicle will provide better cover the long way, with the engine block acting as an effective bullet stop. You can also use the engine block—or better still, the tires—to provide sideways protection. Kneel next to the wheel arch, preferably at the front of the vehicle because the projectiles have to go through more layers of material to get to you than anywhere else on the car.

Be ready to move the instant you become aware the shooter is breaking down the angles and you no longer have the benefit of dead ground.

Bullets travel in a straight line, so always move at an angle off the line of fire

This can be accomplished by using the Ten to Two rule. Keep moving away from the shooter's Ten to Two: out of his sharply focused line of sight into his peripheral vision and then out of sight.

In the street there are stone or brick walls, street corners providing dead ground, crash barriers, and curbs. Dumpsters provide excellent cover. In fact, there is an endless variety of architectural and urban street furniture. Use these features and keep moving from one to another as you find it necessary. Stay low. Move fast.

In a holiday beach situation, try to move away from the gunfire but move at an angle, which will take you to protective covers. Covers may include sand dunes, rocky outcrops, or a promenade with architectural features to shield you.

There are good reasons why the military uses sandbags for cover. One foot of sand can take the kinetic energy out of heavy rounds. Look for impressions or hollows in the beach in which to take cover.

I would personally avoid trying to swim to safety. I know of at least two waterside terror events where active shooters strafed those attempting to swim for safety with automatic rifle fire.

However, depending on the prevailing circumstances, your decision may be different. You may have assessed that the shooter is moving away from the water and you might then choose to swim. If you haven't been seen, and you can make it to the water, swimming may be a good option.

Many people have successfully survived an active shooter event by pretending to be dead and therefore no longer warranting the killer's attention.

Frequently, the person who is playing possum may already have been wounded, making their fall to the ground absolutely authentic. Others have not been wounded but have been in the general arc of fire. They fall to the ground and play lifeless.

Once you have committed to this course, you pretty much have to stay with it. I would advise you make your "death" look authentic and do not fall over too dramatically.

If at all possible, try to fall out of sight and into cover. If you fall near anyone else, try not to drop next to wounded people who are conscious and moaning. The shooter may return to finish them off—and you too in the process.

If you are near blood, discreetly smear some on your clothes and face. This may seem gross and disrespectful but this is about survival. I'm sure victims wouldn't mind donating some blood so that others might live.

Helping others

All government buildings, universities, schools, hospitals, and many private buildings open to the public have wheelchair access. If a wheelchair is available, you can use it to help others escape if they are not as mobile—children, the elderly, the injured or disabled. Same rules of cover apply. Quickly go in the opposite direction of the gunfire, and take cover where appropriate for your situation.

Adrenaline will help you. Once you build up momentum, you can—and will—be able to keep up with the pack.

Older children will be terrified and need to be calmed as best as possible. You may be tempted to hide small infants in cupboards. I strongly recommend avoiding this recourse.

Keep children with you. If the active shooter closes in on you, it may be necessary to use yourself as a living decoy for the sake of your children. These are split-second decisions.

Frail, underweight folk can be easily carried. A fireman's carry, where you take a person over your shoulder, or a piggyback, can be most effective. But if you have unmotivated people who refuse to go on, leave them where they are. This is an unfortunate and distressing reality, but necessary in order to have any chance yourself.

Using your cell phone, and without compromising your personal safety, pass on as much information to the authorities as you can on a regular basis. That means don't break cover to act as a forward spotter for the police. It's too risky.

Police may already be aware that an armed incident is underway, in which case the emergency operator will probably ask you questions to which they don't yet have answers.

In general, they will want to know your name. They will want an exact location. They will want to know how many shooters may be present and, if you have seen them, their descriptions.

They will want to know what weapons are involved. Don't waste time trying to identify what they are if you don't have that knowledge. Just say what you can about them.

Handgun or rifle? Long bursts of fire or short ones? Those details will be extremely useful for police or Special Forces deploying to the scene.

If you have the presence of mind, tell them the general direction in which the incident is developing. An estimate of the increase in the number of casualties will also assist with their response

All the while, keep moving and keep looking for cover. Rest and regroup in any good cover you have found. But be ready to move in an instant.

A police dispatcher may ask you to stay on the line. You have to judge whether that will put you in any further danger.

Remember: You shouldn't wait to be murdered. Not even while holding on the line for the police.

* * *

Situational Awareness and Dynamic Risk Assessment will give you the observational skills to scope out as many exits as possible in your situation, not just the official emergency exits.

Soft cover keeps you out of sight but doesn't afford bullet protection.

Hard cover affords a degree of protection from bullets—concrete, steel, and very thick wood.

Dead ground is a position out of the shooter's field and angles of fire.

Stay low and move fast whenever you move within a shooter's orbit

Remember the Ten to Two rule and utilize it at all times. Always attempt to stay out of the shooter's line of sight.

Do not be one of the herd. Lead, follow, or get out of the way!

If at all possible, **help children, the aged, and the disabled.**

Use your cell phone to assist law and order forces only when it is safe to do so! Otherwise stay off it!

Chapter Four

DISRUPTION

In this chapter, I will outline ways and means of disrupting the progress of an active shooter. I'll tell you how everyday items and street furniture can be used to set traps and pitfalls for the killer. I will show you how to impede his progress and create uncertainty to unsettle him psychologically.

The previous chapters have prepared you for what's coming next. Let's assume that you've been unable to escape the killing zone wherever it may be situated—mall, hotel, airport, or nightclub.

You've been successfully using cover and concealment to protect yourself from active shooters. I'll assume, too, that you've been using your skills of Situational Awareness and Dynamic Risk Assessment. These will provide you with the real-time, rolling critiques of your situation.

Your path to safety may be effectively blocked by the presence of one or more active shooters positioned between you and a route out of the killing field. You've assessed the situation, and that's what you've concluded: no escape. What now? The time has come to again apply your baseline question and ask . . . what if?

What if I stay where I am? If you think it's probable the active shooter is going to run you down and murder you, then the answer is to move. You have to vacate that position.

The time has come to make a tactical retreat further into the shooting zone to put distance between you and the killer. However, do not despair. If you act decisively, you can do this in a way that will cause maximum disruption for the active shooter and significantly hamper and disrupt his activities.

The military defines the doctrine of disruption as attacks and obstacles designed to upset the tempo of an enemy's offensive, to punctuate his timetable, and to cause him to attack in a piecemeal way.

That's pretty much what you're aiming to do. You want to delay and interrupt his murder schedule; you want to make life difficult and, if possible, dangerous for him, too.

You can do this adequately if you are acting on your own. If you have managed to gather a small group of other like-minded folk around you, then you can multiply the effects. Remember, the average length of time a shooting event lasts is eight minutes, and 37 percent in the United States last less than five minutes.

Delay and disruption rob the killer of seconds. Seconds count. Seconds add up. The longer you delay him by disruption, the more likely armed law enforcement officers will arrive to intervene.

The active shooter has certain aims and expectations. His aim is to spook the herd into a stampede and pick them off at will. He expects to be the top predator in the location. He expects a clear arc of fire in front of him as he picks off the stragglers from the herd. He expects to dominate.

What he does not expect is a fight from individuals who've broken away from the herd. He doesn't expect disruption so effective that it actually restricts his arcs of fire.

Remember: you are not one of the herd! You will respond first with disruption. Later, if you have no other choice, you will respond with intense violence to defend yourself and others.

Evasion and disruption come before fighting back. They are the first elements of a counterattack and you should pursue them aggressively.

Fill the path with obstacles

First, take off in a direction that leads away from the sound of gunfire. As you move, leave a trail of obstruction behind. Throw chairs in the path behind you. If there are stores, bars, or restaurants on your way, grab bottles and smash them on the ground in the mall or the street.

Set off fire alarms. Some experts are not sure about the value of this strategy, citing the possibility that people barricaded in rooms will leave them, fearing a blaze has started, and then run into the shooter. I don't think so. I believe those folks would wait for other signs, such as smoke, before they believed there was a real fire.

However, the noise of the alarms will be disconcerting and distracting to the active shooter. It will also make it almost impossible for him to listen for more victims. Personally, I would set off alarms.

If you can activate fire sprinkler systems, do so. You may need a smoke or heat source to do this. A cigarette lighter would do. Water pouring on him will slow the shooter down. The downpour will also blur and disrupt his vision, making it more difficult to fire his weapon accurately.

Wet floors are slippery floors. The active shooter will be slowed down by water on the surfaces. These effects may only be marginal, but they will be significant.

Seconds count during an attack, and if you keep shaving seconds off the killer's effective firing time, you are robbing him of victims.

You are also delaying the time before he reaches your location or the locations of other innocents hiding from him. Delaying tactics are effective tactics.

Split seconds represent lives during a shooting event!

In chapter three, I urged you to take particular note of janitor facilities and premises with kitchens. There are two reasons for this. The first is that janitors and kitchens are both likely to have quantities of soap and cleaning products on hand. Restaurants and kitchens will also have products such as olive oil and cooking oil in usable quantities.

You can make good use of these everyday products. Especially in a situation like a mall or a nightclub, an airport or a theater—anywhere with marbled or tiled, uncarpeted floors—these products can be very useful.

Deploy these products between your position and the direction the killer is likely to come from. Simply throw them across the floor in as wide a spread as possible to create a slip zone.

As he enters this area, the shooter is going to feel, at the very least, unstable on his feet. There's a chance he might actually slip and fall. Just making him feel unsafe on his feet is going to achieve important goals in your disruption strategy.

It will upset the tempo and rhythm of his shooting. For instance, his ability to turn quickly to locate fresh targets will be considerably hindered. Not having a stable firing platform is very disconcerting for any shooter. It will also slow his reload ability as he has to consciously "feel his feet" before he changes magazines.

This instability during a reload could become crucial in any attempt to disarm and attack the shooter. I'll explain this further in the next chapter.

The killer is now facing a new set of issues that are working against him. He has to deal with weaving his way around chairs scattered about and broken glass under his feet, a destabilizing slip zone, getting drenched from water sprinklers, and being distracted by the reverberations of alarm bells.

These unexpected factors are going to delay his timetable, which means precious seconds are knocked off his killing schedule. Remember: seconds mean lives.

Your slip zone is essentially a booby trap and if the killer runs onto it, completely loses his footing, and falls, then the trap has worked perfectly. At the very least he will have lost even more time, and his tempo of killing will have been seriously affected.

With luck, he may even hurt himself in the fall. A sprained ankle or an injured wrist or arm would be perfect. If he's knocked his head, that's good news, too.

Such a turn of events may even present you, and those with you, the perfect moment to completely turn the tables and attack the shooter.

Collect weapons

This brings me immediately to the second reason for raiding the contents of a janitor's closet or a kitchen. Both of these places provide an abundance of very effective weapons.

A janitor's supply room is likely to have quantities of bleach and caustic cleaning materials on hand that can be used for blinding, in addition to anything from broom handles to copper pipes that can be used as clubs.

Corrosive cleaning materials can be used to attack an active shooter by throwing or pouring them over him, perhaps from a gallery above. They will burn and blind. The effects will frighten and disorient him. His shooting tempo may be drastically curtailed if not completely stopped because of the effects to his eyes.

If the opportunity arises, throw caustic liquids directly into his face. A janitor is likely to also have a mop on hand. Improvise. A mop soaked in bleach suddenly smacked into a shooter's face in a surprise attack will have a serious effect on his ability to continue an attack.

He will be blinded and his skin will burn. It may well be the start of the end for him. I will say more about this and other attack strategies in the next chapter.

It may be you already have pepper spray or Mace in your possession. Many people, especially women, buy and carry these self-defense products as protection against attack in the street.

Products such as Mace or pepper spray have tried-and-tested ranges and effects. They fire quite accurately in the direction at which you aim. They could prove indispensable when turned against an active shooter. If you are carrying one, prepare to use it on the killer if the opportunity arises.

If you are not confident about using your spray on a shooter and you have teamed up with others, then volunteer it to the person who has assumed leadership of the group. If he or she has read this book they will already be formulating a plan involving a group attack on the assailant, and weapons will be needed.

Wherever possible, use your natural ingenuity to make improvised weapons on the spot. If you can adapt, you can win. Faced with a desperate situation, your mind will be racing; you will find uses for the materials on hand that you would never have imagined otherwise.

Kitchens are probably the best places to find weapons. They are usually equipped with a whole range of knives and cleavers, some of them large and capable of inflicting serious, life-threatening wounds. As with the janitor's closet, they store caustic cleaning materials and bleach, too.

If you can access a kitchen, collect all that you can carry. If you are part of a small team of people, then you'll be able to act in concert and equip yourselves with a considerable quantity of weaponry.

I can't overstate the effectiveness of a knife or cleaver in combat. Even without any training, an average person can cause devastating damage with such a weapon. Grab one and slip it into your belt.

A broken glass or bottle gives you a jagged-edged blade that can be just as effective. There are many hard plastic items with strong points, which can be used to stab.

A club is also an effective weapon, so grab anything that may be used as a baton to inflict blunt trauma on the shooter should the opportunity arise.

Again, keep your eyes and your mind open to the possibilities of everyday objects being adapted into weapons of lethal force. A sports store will have baseball bats. A hardware store will be filled with countless lethal objects from chisels to scythes. Many of them sell equipment with long handles such as pitchforks. Such a tool used as a lance could deliver a lethal wound.

One of the most useful objects you can acquire will be a fire extinguisher. Prominently located in public places, they are usually stored behind glass, which can be broken with a shoe. Quite often, a fire hose reel is also located with them. We've all seen these assemblages.

They generally come in two types: dry chemical and foam. When activated, the dry chemical extinguisher emits a large cloud designed to envelop and knock out small fires before they take hold.

The foam extinguisher delivers a drenching burst of wet chemical foam. Both are blinding and irritating.

If at all possible, take possession of an extinguisher and add it to your armory of potentially offensive weapons. I will go into details of how to best deploy fire extinguishers in the next chapter.

At the start of this book I gave a broad overview of the problems and issues facing victims when confronted by active shooters. I mentioned that I don't particularly concern myself with the motives of the active shooter, only with his methods and how you can counter them.

This still largely stands. However, in the context of the disruption of the shooter's activities, I think it's appropriate to make a distinction between the profile of the college campus type of killer and the jihadist.

It's more than likely that the paranoid shooter, intent on avenging real or imagined slights from his community, will have played and replayed the scenario in his mind. He may want the event to unfold in a particular way. He will have savored his revenge in his dreams.

I doubt whether he will have factored noise, soaking sprays of water, broken glass, etc. into his multiple-murder fantasy. Not having it play out in the way he imagined in his dreams may well disorient him. Disruptive tactics are likely to be more effective against this type of attacker.

The jihadi may have had some training that might help him stay focused on his mission more successfully. But disruption is still a major factor in undermining any attack on any battlefield, and a terror attack is just that.

It's also worth noting that the classic domestic mass shooter and a jihadi assassin may both be under the influence of drugs. Paranoid killers may be influenced by psychotic medication. Jihadists are known to use amphetamines and cocaine.

For our purposes there's no point in considering their psychology in depth. Just bear in mind that the disruptive techniques we are discussing here may have a significant destabilizing effect on the psyche and decision-making processes of both classes of shooter.

Remember: We can and will fight back if we must.

* * *

If you cannot escape the killing zone, move away from the shooter while causing the maximum amount of disruption possible.

Disruption is defined as attacks and obstacles designed to upset the tempo and timetable of an offensive. That's your objective.

As you evade and retreat from imminent danger, hurl furniture, smash glasses and bottles in a shooter's path. Set off fire alarms and activate sprinkler systems.

Throw olive oil, lubricating oil, or liquid detergents and soaps in his path to create a slip zone. Raid kitchens, janitor's cupboards, hardware stores, etc. for weapons. Collect acid or caustic cleaning liquids, too.

Fire extinguishers may prove to be invaluable in any rush attack on the assailant. Find one if you can! Muster any patented, manufactured self-defense products, such as Mace, pepper spray, or a laser flashlight.

Chapter Five

CONFRONT AND ATTACK

In this chapter, I will discuss the issues involved with the vexed question of confronting and attacking an armed shooter. I will show you how this can be done and how to organize yourself and others. I will describe different strategies for different scenarios, whether you're trapped in a room or on the run in a mall. It is possible to take a shooter down. Remember, all options are open. A determined individual or group can achieve anything.

This chapter undoubtedly poses the toughest questions you will have to face if you are swept up in a terror event. Do you attack or not? When should you attack? And, crucially, *how* should you attack an active shooter?

For the purposes of this chapter I am going to assume you are unarmed in the conventional sense. By that, I mean you are not legally in possession of a pistol with a concealed carry permit. The options, techniques, and potential pitfalls of a concealed carry response to an active shooter will be discussed at length in the chapter seven.

In any event, these are split-second decisions. If you are determined and confident, then you will act immediately. If you are in mortal fear of life and limb, the solutions will come instinctively.

The law allows you to inflict extreme force on an assailant until he is subdued and disarmed, at which point you must stop and simply restrain him. Essentially, that means you can kill him while disarming him but not after he's been disarmed. I'm sure thousands of lawyers will offer different opinions on that, but you have to do what you have to do in the heat of the moment.

I want to tell you what I believe the nature of your response should be in one word. That word is medieval. Most of you will have seen movies such as *Braveheart* that depict the utter violence of a medieval battlefield.

Get medieval

If you get the chance of taking on an active shooter, you must approach the task in the same manner. Be prepared to put forth all your terror, loathing, and need to survive into a few seconds of extreme violence. You must channel and target that aggression into effective action.

Attack the back of the head—as low as possible—smashing into the soft occipital bone at the base of the skull. It can be deadly, and at the very least it will definitely cause instant debilitation.

If you're a little lower than that, with relatively little force it is possible to break his cervical vertebrae, the portion of the spine right below the skull, maximizing injury and possibly causing instant paralysis.

Or go for the face. The best target is the bridge of the nose, just under the nose, or the throat. Think soft tissue, again with maximum violence and blunt trauma force to debilitate, disorient, and blind the killer.

Then you have to stamp on the back of his knees to take him down with every intention of rendering him unable to walk again. Determine that once he's down, he's never getting up again.

Damaging a shooter's sight will rob him of the ability to aim and cause more death and injury. Gouge at his eyes if you have to. Don't hesitate to burn out his sight with hot drinks or caustic cleaning substances. Remember, if he should somehow regain domination over you, he will use his eyes to aim his weapon again.

Similarly, his arms and hands control the weapon. He needs those limbs to cradle and turn his weapon in your direction. Disable them with extreme violence to prevent him from regaining control of his gun.

He uses his fingers to correctly position and hold the gun with precision, to change magazines, and ultimately to pull the trigger. Snap his fingers, stamp on his hands, slash and stab them with a blade if you have to.

It may be that you cannot immediately get to those key body parts. If that's the case, then cause severe damage to any other part of his body you are able to reach. A blunt trauma to the collarbone, for instance, will paralyze him down that side temporarily.

A lot of people may be casting about looking for an effective weapon without realizing they have one over their shoulder. It's your book bag or computer bag. It contains everything from your laptop to your lunch and usually weighs several pounds.

Swung on its long strap, the laws of physics turn your book bag into a fantastic modern version of the medieval ball and chain. It is quite capable of stunning an attacker or knocking him out. You can use it to assault an active shooter. A briefcase swung at the head of an attacker is a good alternative.

However, if you have no available weapon to inflict blunt trauma, I will explain the best ways to disarm a shooter. To do so, you have to understand the mechanics of a shooter's grip on his weapon.

The firing hand, whether left or right, holds a rifle or pistol in a way that's designed to let the shooter point it in the direction he wants to shoot and to pull the trigger.

The other hand is used to add stability by supporting the firing hand in the case of a pistol, or by supporting the long barrel in the case of a rifle. This is not a vise-like grip; it is just strong enough to control the weapon.

In the case of both a rifle and a handgun, the shooter is totally vulnerable to any attempt to force his weapon upward. If this is done with power and determination, he cannot resist it.

If you attempt to force his weapon downward, he is able to exercise more grip and mechanical force against you, which can end in a dangerous wrestling match for control of the weapon.

Understanding this, come at a shooter from his flanks if at all possible, and do so with utter determination. Exploit a shooter's inherently weak grip with Speed, Aggression, and Surprise—SAS—and you will be successful.

Grab the weapon by the barrel, with both hands in the case of a rifle, and force it violently upward. If you are attacking from the right, twist the weapon viciously to the right. Slam your hip into his body as you do so and he will have to release the weapon.

Remember, active shooters constantly have their finger on the trigger. As you are pulling the weapon upward and twisting it in one explosive and violent movement, he will either let go of his weapon or his finger will break against the trigger guard.

Once you have the weapon, use it against him. Shoot him with it or use it as a club to bludgeon his head until he is neutralized.

Remember:

- Always force a weapon upward with maximum power.
- Twist the weapon as you do so, and smash your hip into the shooter's body.
- He will be forced to release his weapon to you.

- Use the weapon to beat his head until he is both disarmed and subdued. Get medieval!

These methods work if you are determined and warlike. If you practice with a replica or deactivated weapon, or in real time on a dry range, you'll discover just how effective these techniques are.

Practice hard and fast with aggression and purpose, but make sure your practice partner never has a finger inside the trigger guard. Trust me, it will be broken.

In an actual terror attack, get medieval and show no restraint until the shooter has been disarmed and subdued. There can be no half measures. Remember, one of the great paradoxes of civilized society is that extreme measures are sometimes required to tackle extremism.

When the shooter can no longer be of danger, stop your attack and restrain him until law enforcement arrives. Ensure that his weapon is completely out of his reach. I would not offer him any medical-first response to the injuries you have inflicted. Who knows, he might sue!

Harden your heart to the shooter's humanity. He's already hardened his to yours.

In addition to determination, what is needed in the midst of a terror event is a plan. Whether it's to escape or attack, you need to come up with one instantly. Once you've read this book, I'm certain it will give you the capabilities you need to make this happen.

Events will be unfolding at a terrific speed. Your plan and its execution could easily be over in the time it takes to read a fraction of this page—in less than a minute from start to finish. For example, I was once in a patrol firefight with terrorists that lasted only four and a half minutes but left several of them dead.

Swarming the shooter

One approach is to swarm or rush the shooter in order to bring him down. This can be very effective and can be achieved by a group or crowd of potential victims all rushing the shooter and immobilizing him with sheer numbers and by the ferocity of the attack.

It works, but more often than not someone will be wounded or killed in the rush. Often, a swarm starts spontaneously when an individual decides enough is enough and goes for it. In one well-documented incident, a seventy-four-year-old ex-US Army colonel was the catalyst for a successful rush attack.

No doubt a shooter will panic when a mob of screaming, furious people bear down on him. He'll know he can't take them all on. It will be his turn to experience fear.

The proximity of people closing on him will restrict his aim and disrupt his kill tempo. This is particularly true with a long-barreled weapon that arcs relatively slowly compared to a handgun.

The Israeli authorities advocate this swarm technique, and it has been used with success there. However, most Israelis have had military training and many have frontline experience. They are used to acting in concert for the greater good. With the increase in random terror attacks in our society, perhaps it's time to take a leaf out of their book.

Swarming works best in an enclosed situation such as a nightclub or a cinema. It can also work well on a plane or train. It works best if people rush the shooter from behind after he has passed them by. A full-frontal assault is likely to end in disaster.

But a shooter will not be able to resist five, ten, fifteen, or twenty people rushing him from behind or from the flanks, all striking at him with blunt or sharp weapons, some of them wrestling his gun away.

There have been videos of large numbers of people, seemingly frozen with shock, standing behind an active shooter during at least two nightclub attacks. They were standing in his Six, and if they'd rushed him from behind they would no doubt have brought the shooter down.

There's no suggestion of any blame on the part of victims who freeze with terror. No one asks to have his or her evening venue shot up. People are shocked and get disoriented, and most don't have any training to fall back on.

However, I like to think that after reading this book, any of you who find yourselves in that situation might be inspired to yell—"Get him!"—and lead the charge.

The swarm is a desperate strategy, but it's proven to work. However, I've seen some ill-advised tactics in a number of videos showing martial arts masters disarming a gunman positioned directly in front of them—right in the shooter's Twelve.

This is usually done with some lightning-fast moves on the shooter's gun-holding wrist or arm. Impressive. Even when you take into account the "shooter" is a student or instructor from the master's dojo or studio.

I've known some Special Forces operatives from the United States and the United Kingdom who've pulled this trick off. But they disarmed gunmen who were in the process of taking them prisoner. The mind-set of their captors was hostile and alert but far more passive than that of an active killer. The terrorist just wants to kill you. Period.

If I told my SF comrades, who've disarmed a gunman face-on, that I was willing to attempt the same with an active shooter, I know they'd smile and say: "Good luck with that, buddy!"

Never try to disarm an active shooter face-on unless there is absolutely no other way!

In hiding

At this point, I want to discuss a specific scenario that has affected thousands of people during active shooter events in the United States and elsewhere. This is the situation where people crowd into a room while an active killer is on the prowl through corridors outside looking for victims.

What if he arrives outside the door you are hiding behind? This was the nightmare thousands of students confronted during events such as Columbine and Virginia Tech, as well as staff in attacks in offices.

I am going to take you step-by-step through the way I would handle this high-terror situation. I know lots of schools and businesses go through the grim necessity of lockdown drills. However, I have a couple of extra pointers that people might find useful.

If you are able to lock a strongly constructed door and effectively barricade the room with sufficiently heavy objects, then all is well and good. Follow the standard advice. Take whatever cover is available. Switch off all lights and appliances in the room such as copying machines. Switch off the sound on cell phones and stay silent.

Do not open the door. Remember the wedge-shaped doorstops used to hold doors open? If you see any, collect every one of them you come across—they're perfect for jamming a door shut, too. Once that's done, barricade the door as well. Lock, jam, barricade.

If you hear someone knocking on the door, pleading for sanctuary, assume it is the shooter trying to fool you. Don't answer. Someone knocking on the door and calling out for you to assist with a wounded person may also be the shooter trying to sucker you. Don't make a sound.

Stay away from the doors. Bullets will go through doors and they will also go through studded walls, so keep flat on the floor with as many layers as possible in between you and the gunfire. Use wooden tables, chairs, computers, photocopiers, freezers, whatever. Dead bodies are fantastic cover. That's just a gruesome fact. Filing cabinets full of paper will stop a round. If they are empty they won't.

If a 7.62 round from an AK-47 goes through a wooden door, a stud wall, and a couple layers of classroom tables, there is a good chance you will not be hit; the rounds will be deflected, disrupted, and ultimately destroyed.

Only exit the room when you are absolutely certain law enforcement officers have taken control of the building. When you do come out, follow their instructions to the letter.

Don't rush toward the officers. They will be pumped up, aggressive, and sometimes unpredictable, depending on their experience; they may have lost comrades, and they may be afraid. At that moment, all you may want to do is hug the cop who saved you. Resist the temptation. All he wants to do at that moment is verify that you're not involved with the shooter in any way.

Kick away any weapons you have amassed and throw up your hands. Assume as passive a stance as possible and scream, "Don't shoot!" The hugs can wait.

Don't be offended if the officers handcuff you until they've given you the okay; that's normal. They are just following the policy laid down by their department's particular standard operating procedures.

The police will also be looking for terrorist "sleepers" who have thrown away their weapons and infiltrated a large crowd with the hope of escape. Unfortunately, in some hostage situations, they will also be looking for terrorists being protected by their victims. "Stockholm syndrome" has happened more than once, and sadly it will happen again.

Let's now turn to a far more difficult situation. You are in a room where the door doesn't lock and nothing is heavy enough to make an effective barricade. You have a problem.

My advice is that you nominate a number of physically robust and confident people as prime assaulters. The rest will fall into a role that is initially diversionary, quickly followed by a second phase of rushing and swarming.

It's a very good idea, once people are nominated for these roles, to practice the techniques I am about to describe. Organize them at your school or workplace as soon as possible.

A school class will be able to identify and nominate the football player or the young woman with a black belt in their midst for the job of initiating the primary attack. The same goes for employees in an office or a business.

However, volunteers and heroes will emerge in all sorts of traumatic situations and there will always be surprises. Some people you thought were jocks may pull back into the shadows, and others you thought of as milquetoasts may take the fight to the enemy.

Here's what should happen if you hear the strange pops and muffled bangs of an active shooter attack. Screams and shouts will also alert you. At this point, immediately enter the drill you should already have practiced.

If the door is centered evenly on the wall, two attackers each should assume positions on either side of the door. One should kneel in front of the other.

If the door is up against the junction of two walls, there will only be room for two attackers to assume this same position on one side of the door.

While the primary attackers are getting in position, the others—the support group—should be busy with their first role, which is to create diversions and distractions.

Once again, this should have already been practiced until it came as second nature and could be performed swiftly and in silence. Do not babble. Ideally there should be one voice—that of the nominated leader. The leader should issue commands and instructions in a stage whisper—audible within the room but not outside.

The first distraction should be visual—in the line of sight of the shooter when he opens the door and enters the room. It should be right in his Twelve to immediately capture his attention.

Public areas like a school campus, factories, and business venues should have plenty of fire extinguishers. Foam and dry chemical types are the best as they create a great distraction to the shooter, as well as a smoke screen that shields you from his view. They will also irritate his eyes and lungs. These are top-grade weapons.

The nominated attackers should position themselves on either side of the door and be armed with at least one extinguisher and whatever else comes to hand or has been collected along the way. Lock, jam, and barricade where possible. In the case of an unlocked door, a barricade will still slow down, disorient, and cause maximum distraction and unease to the shooter.

The remainder of the group should create a multilayered barricade utilizing all the contents of the office or classroom and get behind it. This barricade needs to be a large solid mass because it's inevitably going to draw fire.

In military terms, the plan goes as follows: Those at the doors are the assaulters. The folk behind the cover are the "fire support" or backup team. The idea is to outflank the enemy.

The shooter bursting in the door springs the ambush. As soon as he attempts entry, the fire extinguisher carriers aim at him. This will immediately create a smoke screen obscuring the gunman's aim. The barricade will obstruct his options for movement.

With the shooter blinded, the assaulters strike with extreme violence. After clubbing his head with the empty extinguishers, they should then grab his weapon with both hands, ripping the gun violently left or right and upward. As described earlier, he will be forced to release it or his finger will be broken.

Simultaneously, the fire support group must rush the assailant and attack with everything they've managed to get their hands on. Anything goes. Club, gouge, and slash.

No fire extinguishers? No problem. Nothing changes. The lights are still switched off and any blinds in the windows come down. When the shooter enters the support group behind heavy cover, scream to draw fire so the assaulters can outflank the killer.

Reflections will also create a good distraction. Ideally, you need something the height of an average person. It should be placed just a couple of steps into the room, and it should be reflective. A mirror grabbed from the restroom would be perfect. If no mirror is available, a computer monitor or a television screen will do.

If nothing reflective is available, then something such as a classroom whiteboard could be wheeled into place or a table stood up on its end in front of the door. When the second group has finished preparations for the diversion, they should move to the prepared multilayered barricade, ready to do their bit.

The idea is that the shooter will be confronted with an object and possibly a reflection staring back at him. He is likely to do a double take and to hesitate. For a split second he will have registered another person directly in his face. He may shoot at this "person" confronting him.

He is unlikely to have yet registered the presence of the assaulters waiting on either side of the door who are already moving in on him. The assault team will go straight for the weapon in his hands. Again, step inside the shooter's arm, grasp his weapon with a vise-like grip, and twist it sharply left or right and upward.

At the same time that the killer's weapon is being targeted, the attacker behind could either stamp on the back of the shooter's knee or dive around his legs to tackle him and bring him down.

The support group will join in and kick, stamp, and smash him. If you've managed to gather blades or broken glass, cut and slash as well. In any case, go to work on him with everything you can deploy.

Remember: Be medieval. Be brutal.

In the open

I'll now go on to discuss a different scenario, one where a shooter is on the rampage in a far more open situation. So far, I've typified this sort of situation with the shopping mall as it contains so many features common to other locations such as airport lounges, hotel complexes, etc.

Once again, I must emphasize that each separate active shooter event takes on a life of its own. There are so many imponderables that it's not possible to offer an entirely standard response. Not least of the random factors is the whimsical nature of a shooter's progress through the urban scape.

Therefore, I can only offer a range of suggestions and tips that you should be able to take and use in a variety of scenarios. The key is to absorb the information I offer so it's available if you ever need to draw on it.

Think on your feet and adapt what you've learned.

The last chapter was about creating diversions, but it must be obvious by now that diversion and attack are really one part of a free-flowing event. They meld into each other in rapid real time. I've only laid them out in different chapters to help the reader.

Imagine you've tried various routes to escape, but through circumstance the shooter is located between you and the exit and has you trapped. However, you've managed to collect some weapons and a group of people have gathered around you.

They are in varying states of physical fitness and ability. Some of them are too distressed mentally to be of much assistance. None of them have any military combat or law enforcement experience. In these circumstances, you have assumed a leadership role.

Your rolling Dynamic Risk Assessment tells you it is probable the shooter will be in your location imminently.

What if he does come your way? You reason that if you don't attack, there's a high probability you and those around you will be killed or wounded. In your judgment, there's no choice but to attempt to take the shooter down.

On the plus side, while attempting to escape, you've collected a substantial armory of makeshift weapons. You've also followed my advice and created diversions on the approaches to your position. You've scattered the area with overturned furniture and broken glass.

You've set off fire alarms and managed to activate the sprinkler system with a chef's blowtorch you found in a kitchen. For good measure, you also set off a jet of water from a fire hose you found while commandeering two extinguishers. You have created a slip zone with various oils and detergent products, too.

The shooter is still coming toward you. You hear shots and screams of pain and panic. First, gather those who, through age, illness, or nerves, can be assigned as noncombatants. Hide them wherever you think they'll be safest.

Do your best for them, but don't waste time on this task. Taking out the killer will be the best favor you can do them. Concentrate on that outcome.

Situational Awareness comes into play as you scan the location for the most suitable place to lay an ambush. Columns and pillars, the corners of corridors, or doorways out of the shooter's line of sight are all good options.

We just went over using reflections against the killer when defending a classroom or office. Wherever possible—in this different scenario—think about using reflections as well.

When hiding in readiness for an ambush, look for a line of sight onto any architectural reflective surface such as plate glass or a large mirror. As you are waiting to attack, a reflection glimpsed on glass will alert you to the killer's approach.

He, on the other hand, will not be looking for reflections but for solid human targets to shoot, which will work to your advantage when the odds are against you.

Remember the principles of dead ground. Remember to protect your Six. You don't want the shooter coming up behind you. That would result in a bad outcome.

Above all, try to find a choke point where the shooter's advance in your direction is narrowed either by the architecture of the building or the slip zone, barricades, or diversions you've created.

If you're with others, deploy yourselves out of sight behind hard cover at a point where the shooter is either walking through the choke point or is just exiting it.

As he comes into sight, immediately attack him from the flanks outside of his Ten to Two. Maximize the attack with whatever makeshift weapon you have. Go for the head, throat, or back of the neck.

Blast the fire extinguishers into his face. Foam or dry chemical, either will burn his eyes and his lungs for a short but crucial period. Both have an effective range of about ten feet. In reality you could and should be a lot closer.

If there are two of you, then both blast extinguishers at him. The attack must be coordinated, at close quarters, from a flank, and with the element of surprise. Immediately follow this attack by smashing him around the head with the empty metal canister.

As with any attack on an active shooter, prosecute it with extreme violence until he can offer no further harm.

Grasp his weapon as previously described, twisting it on his trigger finger and wrist so he is forced to release it. Continue your attack by whatever means until the shooter is no longer capable of attack, and then retain his weapon.

Both pepper spray and Mace are excellent weapons as well. If they are not available, you might have caustic cleaning products to throw in his face. A surprise blinding of the assailant is a good first move. Follow it with a burst of extreme violence.

If you cannot identify a choke point for an ambush, then hide, and as he passes move into his Six, swiftly deploying your weapons as soon as you come upon him.

You will be surprised at just how close you can come up behind a person before they hear you even in a reasonably quiet environment. That's another function of our predatory nature. We were designed to hear better in front of us than behind because while pursuing quarry we don't expect to be followed.

Think how many times a cyclist has surprised you as they have swept past without being heard. In the killing zone with screams and alarm bells, a shooter is unlikely to hear you until it's too late . . . for him. Stay low, move fast, and charge him down with medieval intensity.

In the case where there's no choke point, you may be more vulnerable to counterattack by the shooter. Rely on speed and ferocity of attack to accomplish your goal of taking him out.

In such a situation, if you're lucky, the shooter may pause to reload his weapon by switching an empty magazine for a full one. Well-drilled soldiers can do this in a couple of seconds.

We know that seconds count, so this will be the ideal moment to set off from your hiding place out of his Ten to Two to ambush him. Don't hesitate. Fortune favors the brave.

Streetscapes usually provide far more opportunities for escape and evasion. Think out of the box for sources of improvised weaponry and fall back onto your drills. Remember your Situational Awareness and Dynamic Risk Assessment. Guard your Six. Constantly move away from the angles of firing. Keep out of range of the shooter's Ten to Two as much as possible. Seek dead ground. In the final analysis, adapt, and try to sneak up behind an active shooter to ambush him with deadly force.

One unfortunate aspect of active shooter events on city streets is that of motorists who inadvertently drive into killing zone. Some have their vehicles shot up while others are killed or wounded behind the wheel.

But I've yet to hear of a driver aiming his vehicle straight at the shooter. If you are in his Ten to Two, you have nothing to lose. He is likely to shoot at you in any event. Pedal to the metal and drive straight at him. Don't slow down.

In a club or theater

The issues surrounding active-shooter attacks at nightclub venues such as the Pulse in Orlando or the Bataclan in Paris are very complex. There are a number of interweaving factors, which make these situations extremely fertile ground for active shooters intent on maximum devastation of life.

Environmental factors can and do exacerbate matters. First, you have the sardine factor. People are jammed in like fish in a can; that's part of the attraction of these venues. There's the noise factor, too. Music, screeches of laughter, shouting—clubs are very loud, which is part of the fun. Strobe lighting throws shadows and colors in mesmerizing patterns around the room; it is all very disorienting.

Because of these factors, people at the Pulse and Bataclan didn't realize they were under attack for several minutes. Once they did, it was too late for many of them. The lighting and the sheer mass of human bodies crammed into a limited space make it extremely difficult to orientate and escape.

Another factor that militates against escape and survival is alcohol and drug consumption. Even if you are relatively sober or straight, it's likely you'll be one of the few.

This is absolutely not a criticism of any of the victims or survivors of the two clubs I've mentioned. They had every right to be out for the night with friends and acquaintances having a drink and a good time.

But I feel it's only right and proper that I should point out the additional challenges created for innocent people in packed, loud, disorienting environments where drink and drugs are involved.

It's precisely why clubs are designated as targets. They are Target-Rich Environments, and in such places, the targets can turn into a swarm.

Similarly, within the confines of a movie theater or a train or airliner, you will be closeted by rows of seating. The only way to end the horror is by swarming the shooter from his Six as soon as he turns his back on you.

He is equally hemmed in by the seats and narrow aisles that are restricting your movement. Remember the drills for disarming a perpetrator and prosecute them with extreme violence.

Confusion and chaos are heightened by the numbers of people in close proximity in a cinema, a train, or a plane. In this sort of environment, I would urge you to rush or swarm the shooter.

He may threaten that he has a bomb. Do you believe him? So what if he does? It just makes a rush attack more pressing. There's everything to lose if you don't. Do it sooner rather than later.

Better to swarm and sting like bees than walk like sheep to the slaughter.

* * *

The vital lessons from this chapter are contained in the drills for disarming a shooter. Practice them.

Always force a shooter's weapon upward. He will not be able to stop you.

Never try to force it down. He will be able to resist and he will bring it back up to shoot you.

A shooter keeps his finger on the trigger. Twist it and he must let go or his finger will break.

Once you have his weapon, use it to shoot him or smash him about the head with it.

You now have the skills. Whatever your situation, whatever the scenario, adapt them to fit and think on your feet. The rest will follow.

Above all, be ruthlessly violent in your counterattack.

Chapter Six

KNIVES

So far, I've obviously concentrated on the outcomes and antidotes of bombings and active shooter events. However, it would be remiss of me to not offer some advice on the increasing danger of random knife attacks.

Knife attacks are most common in Europe where Islamists use knives and machetes in attempted and actual beheadings on the streets, in cafés, in subway stations, on trains, and even at the altars of churches. They have spread to the United States and there's no reason to doubt they will increase in frequency. Neither is there any reason to shy away from the challenge.

You need to have some basic knowledge on how to best defend yourself from knife attacks and turn the tables on the attacker. Knives and machetes are vicious and dangerous weapons that can inflict serious hemorrhagic wounds on the victim. This short chapter should help you defend yourself from them.

The first thing I want to remind you about is that common item carried by millions of people in the streets—the book bag or computer bag. It's heavy and can make a devastating weapon. When danger threatens, don't forget it's there on your shoulder ready to be deployed.

Use it to keep a knifeman at bay or, if you come from his Six or his flank, smash him on the head with it. A briefcase swung at the head of an attacker works, too.

The commonly accepted wisdom about defending yourself from a knife attack is to wrap a jacket around your arm to use it as a crude shield against lunges and slashes.

This is not a good idea. In a knife attack, your aim should be to keep distance between yourself and the blade. Wrapping your arm immediately puts you in a negative, defensive position. By definition, the attacker can get within your arm's length because you are holding it across your body.

The closer he is, the more likely he will be able to get at your throat or chest cavity and heart, which could be fatal. If he slashes around the inside of the elbow, which you will be presenting unwrapped by the jacket, you are likely to suffer catastrophic bleeding from a major vessel.

The best tactic is to run away. But if you are cornered, hold a bag or a briefcase at arm's length with both hands to parry thrusts and slashes. Move side to side as you counter the blows aimed at you. Avoid moving backwards because, sooner or later, you are going to fall over something, allowing the attacker to come above you and attack.

Another everyday item on hand that can be used as a very effective weapon against a knife attacker or a shooter is a coffee cup. As people go about their daily lives, millions hold their cups of coffee as they walk the streets. Hurled into the perpetrator's face, a hot drink will scald and blind him. Follow with a violent attack until he is disarmed.

Several knife attacks have taken place at cafés and bistros. If everyone hurled hot drinks at the knifeman, it would be all over for him. Cold drinks are good, too. Just throw them in his face, especially if they come in a good volume like a beer. Liquid—of any sort—in the face is a big impediment to action.

Follow it up by hurling anything heavy—anything not bolted down—at him. Aim for the head to inflict blunt trauma.

Whenever possible, go for the head.

Table umbrellas are likely to be at a street café. Pull them off the table and they become lances. They can be used to hold the knife-wielding person at bay and inflict serious injury on him. Go for the face and torso.

One of the most useful weapons in a knife-attack scenario is a chair or stool. Hold it in front of you and parry the blows. The knifeman then has a problem because he cannot get his blade close to you. He can't pull the chair out of your vise-like grip with one hand, and he's not ever likely to put his weapon down to engage in a tug of war over it.

If two or more of you are wielding stools and chairs, you can corral a terrorist into a corner or against a wall. Hurl bottles, bags, or bricks at him to inflict injury and deplete his capability of doing harm.

Ideally, while the perpetrator's movement is severely limited in this way, try to come from his flank to inflict blunt trauma with a heavy object. That will bring the terror event to a swift conclusion.

Once again, the aim is to end the attack with controlled violence using sound techniques. It is no use pussyfooting around with anyone wielding a knife.

Chairs work, book bags work, bottles and umbrella shafts work, too. These methods have been tried and tested. Use them.

* * *

When a knife-wielding assassin confronts you, remember to utilize your book bag or briefcase.

Don't wrap a jacket round your arm as a shield. Better to fend him off with a bag, case, or chair at arm's length.

A hot drink will scald him. Look for a fire extinguisher. As always, attack his head if possible from his Six or his flank.

Chapter Seven

I HAVE A GUN TOO!

In this chapter, I'll discuss the best practice and techniques for those of you with a concealed carry permit. This naturally assumes you are packing at the time of an incident. I will explain what you have to do and how to do it. I will also explain protocols for ensuring you are not confused with the perpetrators by law enforcement officers.

Maybe it's not a shooter but a bomber who has been unmasked near you. I'll give you some advice on using your firearm in that circumstance. I will also give some advice for anyone who disarms and takes possession of a shooter's weapon.

So you have a handgun and you believe you can use it proficiently and effectively. Perhaps you can—on the range. Then the completely unexpected happens and you are caught up in an active shooter event.

You are not on the range!

The intensity of the challenge between the two circumstances is vast. Yes, you may be a good shot on the range, but you and others around you are in grave danger.

You may think you have the answer in a holster, but believe me, many people faced with such extreme circumstances go to pieces. All the carefully trained protocols of the range can evaporate in the face of danger.

The first major hurdle you have to overcome is safety. Everything you have previously learned is about not shooting a human but shooting a target, which represents a human.

Suddenly, you are confronted with the necessity to put rounds into living flesh and blood. However odious that person may be, it is a critical moment for the legal bearer of arms.

I know everyone who carries a sidearm is certain they would be able to deploy it in a crisis. "I wouldn't carry if I wasn't prepared to use it," they typically say.

Truth is, that's easier said than done, although I believe that most legal carriers have already done their soul searching and would be able to shoot a perpetrator. Whether they'll be able to use their weapon with their usual proficiency is the big question, and many will freeze or fumble.

Let's look at the problems you'll face and the strategies you should use in more detail. The first thing I want to emphasize is that the most effective use of your handgun will be the discharging of as many rounds as possible into the perpetrator.

I watch people with two or three targets firing two or three rounds into one, turning, repositioning, then firing two or three rounds into the next target, and so on.

But what you're likely to be confronted with is just one person on the rampage with a powerful weapon. So practice putting as many rounds into one target as possible because that's what you will most likely need to do to with a shooter. Empty your magazine into him.

The next, absolutely vital, operation is to change magazines smoothly under extreme pressure. It's easy to fumble this procedure at the worst possible moment when hurrying because of fear. Practice the reload time and time again until it becomes second nature.

When you have reloaded your weapon, fire at the shooter again if he is still standing. Even if he has dropped his weapon, you don't know whether he can pick it up again. This is no time for niceties. You must ensure he presents no further danger.

These are the basic skills you will need to practice on the range if you are ever to confront an active shooter successfully.

Learn to apply sustained fire onto one target. Learn to reload your weapon without fumbling. Fire again.

Practice these skills. It is especially vital you are able to change the magazine smoothly. The magazine change is a moment of vulnerability. It when an active shooter will be the most vulnerable to attack and it's the moment a concealed-carry individual will be the most vulnerable to the shooter.

Practice until it's so ingrained you will not freeze or fumble.

Let's assume you have mastered these skills and are carrying a legally permitted handgun. In most cases it will probably be a semi-automatic. Let's assume you have a handgun powerful enough to effectively counterattack.

Circumstances will vary enormously from attack to attack, and events will unfold at a lightning-fast pace. Following are some simple rule-of-thumb strategies, which will help you enormously if a shooter strikes.

When to use your weapon

The first and most important skill of concealed carry is learning when to draw your weapon. This is a more difficult proposition than you first imagine. The problem is that as soon as you show your handgun, you will immediately attract attention to yourself. That may be very unwelcome indeed.

Potential victims around you may believe you are one of the perpetrators. You may find yourself rushed, swarmed, and severely battered by individuals determined to bring anyone with a firearm down.

You could first call out that you're carrying but, obviously, only do that if you are certain the shooter can't hear you, too.

If you haven't done that, my advice is to keep the sidearm holstered if you are confident enough of a smooth drawing and firing action. If you're not so confident, then take it out and conceal it behind your back, in your pocket, or under your jacket. Keep it locked and loaded.

If you are going to confront the killer, you may find yourself struggling against a human tide fleeing in the opposite direction. It's best not to expend energy swimming against this tide. Instead, move to a flank and find suitable cover. Wait in a position of ambush until you catch sight of the killer. Remember the tactical clock and the Ten to Two rule.

The other, very real danger is from law enforcement, both during the active shooter event and at its end. The police will consider anyone carrying a firearm as a potential killer. If they see a weapon in your hand, they are likely to deal with you summarily and with lethal force.

There is absolutely no point shouting out that you've got a concealed carry permit. They will not be inclined to say, "Okay, guys, we'll have a look at this person's permit first." They'll just shoot you.

The obvious thing to do when law enforcement arrives on the scene is to throw your weapon to one side and hold your hands up, clearly showing they're empty.

The details can be sorted out later. It is be best if you keep quiet and only speak to answer their questions. Do not annoy them with rambling explanations. They will be pumped up and looking out for any threats, so the last thing they'll need is you sounding off.

Also keep in mind that possession of a handgun does not oblige you to immediately confront the shooter or to confront him at all. If you are able to escape and evade, that might be your preferred choice. No shame in that.

If, however, you decide you must take action, consider your situation. Once again, this is where your real-time, rolling risk assessment comes into play.

You will be processing a lot of information. What weapon is the killer deploying: long barrel or pistol? Is he wearing any body armor? What's his demeanor? Is he firing crazily, wasting his ammunition, or is he more calculated?

You will sense instantly whether he's trained or not by the amount of damage he is inflicting. As long as he can't see you, he can't kill you. Stay focused.

Another factor to be considered, particularly in terrorist-related incidents, is that the shooter or shooters may have an extra pair of eyes in the form of an accomplice acting as a spotter.

This is believed to have been the case in some mass killings in Europe. The spotter's role will be to alert the killers to the arrival of police or the presence of any other armed intervention or resistance at the scene. That means you.

You may be in a situation where you cannot escape the area or no cover is available, in which case you must use your weapon immediately. This is the only time I would recommend a face-to-face shoot-out. There's no choice. It will be do or die.

Come from behind and get close

Then again, you may be in a situation where you do have some room to maneuver. If that is the case, start to move from cover to cover as discussed in chapter three. All the while, work to stay out of the shooter's Ten to Two.

Your ultimate goal is to outflank the shooter. If you can get to his Six, that would be optimal. Shoot him in the back. This is not a duel. You are not Doc Holliday. Fire as many rounds as possible into his back. If he's wearing body armor, then aim for his lower back.

Get as close as you can before opening fire. If you're close enough for an accurate head shot, go for that. If you're caught out on a flank, get as close as you can and aim for the center of his body mass. Your goal is to shatter his spinal cord and totally disable him.

He's very unlikely to hear you if you come from directly behind. However, he may have the benefit of reflections from glass or shining metal in the architecture of the location. So, the moment you see him turning, begin to fire and keep shooting into his body mass.

Inexperienced individuals firing accurately in a combat situation from twenty yards would be exceptional. Get much closer. Obviously, there are dangers with that strategy, but firing at the limit of your accurate range and not striking the shooter is a lot more dangerous.

No perpetrator ever died from a fast miss; take the extra second to make the shot count.

Remember that you are not dealing with static, paper targets on a range. The active shooter will be moving. You must get near him to close down his arcs of fire and enable you to instantly adjust your position to take him down.

In most cases, an active shooter is likely to have some sort of long-barrel assault rifle with a longer killing range than yours. If he can, he'll turn it on you. That's yet another reason to get close and, when you are ready, empty your magazine into his body mass.

You will not freeze. Take the shot.

Fire and move. Fire and move. Look at the breach. Slide to the rear. Change the magazine quickly.

You will not fumble the reload.

While you are reloading, observe your left and right constantly. Has the perpetrator been neutralized? Does he still have hands on his weapon? If so, shoot him again.

If you believe he has been rendered "safe," move his weapon away from him. Slide or kick it away, but do not pick it up if law enforcement officers are anywhere near. If there is more than one shooter and you know how to use his more powerful weapon, then do so.

Check if he's wearing what appears to be an explosive vest. Treat any backpack with extreme caution. It might contain an Improvised Explosive Device.

If you believe he has explosives, don't touch the device. Leave the area immediately, warning others to also leave. At the first possible opportunity tell law enforcement you suspect a bomb is present.

Remember: You're a wolf and you can bite back.

* * *

An armed intervention on your part needs control and calculation. Practice on the range to become proficient at putting several shots into one target. Keep practicing the reload, as this needs to be performed smoothly.

Be sure you are shooting at the perpetrator. In the confusion of an actual event, this may not be as clear as you might think.

Keep your weapon in your pocket or at your side to avoid being mistaken for a perpetrator. When law enforcement arrives, ditch your weapon, stay still, and clearly hold your empty hands above your head. Officers will be nervous and potentially lethal.

Chapter Eight

FIRST RESPONSE

Learn how to assist the wounded and use battlefield triage. Make life-or-death decisions and learn how to administer frontline medical aid using accessible materials. If medical packs, defibrillators, etc., are available nearby, that's a bonus. I'll show you how to improvise, adapt, and overcome.

In many ways, this chapter is the most important simply because the information it contains is likely to be of the most use to the most people. In the event you are caught up in a bombing or active shooter event and survive relatively unscathed, what follows in this chapter could save the lives of others.

For the purposes of this chapter, I am going to assume that you are familiar with the techniques of cardiopulmonary resuscitation (CPR) and know how to follow the instructions of any in situ defibrillator. Everyone should be. If you aren't, go to a class and learn CPR procedures as soon as you can.

Any level of first aid training is always a useful skill to have. First aid saves lives. However, in the extreme carnage created by a bomb or a mass shooting, the usefulness of standard first aid training is limited.

What you'll need in the aftermath of a bombing or an active shooter event is a military take on treating casualties. The set of injuries you'll be confronted with will be very different from what you experience in everyday life.

Expect battlefield conditions

A bombing leaves an array of traumatic amputations, devastating shrapnel wounds, and clinical shock. An active shooter inflicts an array of gunshot wounds with entry and exit traumas. Assault rounds track through the body, deflecting off harder bone to lacerate soft tissue and internal organs.

In short, you will be dealing with battlefield injuries, and the skills you need to deal with these visually distressing and medically daunting scenes are designated as Tactical Combat Casualty Care by the US Army.

Combat medical courses are available outside the military, which are usually taken by ex-military personnel wishing to work as protection officers in hostile zones. Anyone can enroll, but they are relatively expensive and greatly in demand. There aren't too many of them with vacancies available.

The particularly high tempo and isolated fighting tasks of Special Forces mean they don't always have access to dedicated medical specialists on operations. The solution was to train some of the SF soldiers in trauma treatment.

I learned those skills and was a designated Patrol Medic, which I utilized along with my other specialties such as sniping and high-altitude parachute insertion into battle. I'm going to give you the benefit of my experience in some basic know-how about battlefield first response.

What you are about to learn will at least enable you to bring order out of chaos and hopefully save lives. I'm not going to pretend anything I tell you can adequately prepare for the aftermath of a violent, warlike event. Military, police, and other first responders will be prepared for what they find, but I've never met one who wasn't shocked to the core after their first time.

You will find the sights, sounds, and smells of the incident profoundly disturbing. You may begin to go into shock. If you feel that happening, pause and follow the measures I outlined in chapter one to bring your faculties back under control. The breathing exercises will prove particularly effective.

You must then be determined to put all squeamishness, distaste, and horror to one side. Get on with the vital task before you.

Don't be fainthearted. Remember: people's lives will be in your hands

Understand that emergency medical services may not be allowed into the danger zone until law enforcement is satisfied the area is safe. They will want to check for secondary devices in the case of a bombing and to be sure no more killers are on the loose in an active-shooting scenario.

It may be an hour or longer before you will see any sign of a paramedic or a doctor. You will have to make do with what you have around you. In the case of the Bataclan nightclub shooting in Paris, for instance, two and a half hours elapsed before professional medics were allowed onto the scene.

Take care of yourself first. If you are in an active-shooter danger zone, keep running and evading. Your first priority is to save yourself. If you are wounded, you can't help anyone else.

After a bomb blast, expect a secondary attack, either another bomb or automatic gunfire. Secondary attacks will be directed at the obvious escape route or choice of cover. So think out of the box. Go for hard cover, not soft cover.

Try to leave the killing zone and, if possible, try to take casualties to a safer position. You may be worried about causing spinal injuries by moving patients, but this is an extraordinary situation. These injuries will be the least of your concerns. In any event, fewer than 5 percent of injuries in bombings and shootings are spinal. However, there is no point moving anyone you do not think will survive.

Prepare to treat the wounded

When you are satisfied that your immediate surroundings are relatively safe, you can begin the task of helping the wounded. Set up a makeshift medical station. Check that the scene is as safe as it can be, out of sight and earshot of the shooters. If the casualty is close to power sources, switch the power off if you are able.

Look for overhanging debris. Is it dangerous? Should you move the casualty or not? When you're satisfied that the area is relatively safe, call out to see if a doctor or a nurse is nearby. If there is, he or she will be invaluable.

Ask around for medical supplies. Someone may have a first aid kit. Everyday items can be of use—female sanitary wear to plug wounds, belts to create tourniquets, etc. Ask for whatever you need. People will shake themselves out of shock and help if they possibly can. That is the human condition.

Triage is a French word meaning to sort out or sift. If a victim is walking, wounded, and yelling for help, that's a good sign. They can wait. In fact, tell them firmly to keep the noise down.

Screaming and shouting will not help you when you are checking vital signs in the very gravely injured or when hoping to avoid attracting the attention of killers.

If you see people with catastrophic bleeding, they need help fast. Talk to the casualties while working at the same time. Ask them their names. Tell them your name. Tell them that you're here to help. Ask their permission to intervene. After all, in the final analysis, it's their body you are working on. It's their life at stake.

If there is no verbal response, proceed with your interventions rapidly. Forget the victim's airway and forget CPR for now. Those issues will soon be dealt with. The priority you must focus and concentrate on is hemorrhage control.

Stop any hemorrhaging

Uncontrolled bleeding is the primary cause of battlefield deaths among soldiers. It is also the major cause of deaths in the aftermath of terror attacks. People with trauma are likely to bleed out very quickly.

Effective hemorrhage control is achieved by the initiation of direct pressure on the wound and by the application of tourniquets. In the case of massive hemorrhage, instantly apply a tourniquet.

Tourniquets and direct pressure work well if the procedures are carried out as confidently and correctly as you can. I know a medical tourniquet is not the kind of everyday product you would have in a handbag or briefcase, but you must improvise.

Think of utilizing belts or briefcase and handbag straps. Panty hose also make a very good alternative.

Immediately provide maximum exposure of the wound site by ripping or cutting clothes away. It is vital that you see the extent of what you are up against; you don't want to miss anything.

In the case of an arm or leg blown off by bomb or bullet, forget the wound and go for the armpit or groin. Position the tourniquet high and tight onto the big bones to trap the severed artery; grab a pen, bolt, stick, or bar to thread under the tourniquet.

Begin twisting the material of the tourniquet using your lever—whatever item it might be—to create a windlass effect to tighten it until the bleeding ceases.

One individual trained in combat medical skills applied at least five tourniquets to casualties with ripped limbs at the Boston Marathon bombing. His interventions saved lives.

The use of tourniquets went out of fashion and were branded a crude intervention for a number of years. But military experience in Afghanistan has proven it to be an effective lifesaver. Deploy a tourniquet where you see spurting blood or where there has been a traumatic amputation.

Again, it should be placed as high as possible on the limb. Quite often, a second one will be needed to completely seal off bleeding. Once the tourniquet is in place, don't try to remove it. It is keeping the casualty alive until the professionals arrive. Removing a tourniquet is a specialized medical procedure.

However, keep checking it. Check that it is still fitted correctly. Check that it is still tight enough to keep the bleeding contained. If it's not doing the job, keep twisting it as tightly as you can.

When bleeding has been arrested and you are satisfied that the patient is not bleeding out, the airway is your next priority.

Keep the patient breathing

No airway equals no life. If you can see mucus, blood, vomit, etc. in a conscious patient, follow this procedure. With one hand supporting the casualty under the neck, the other hand goes to the other side of the body and grasps. Pull the patient toward you so that you effectively turn the patient over and drain the airway.

If the casualty is unconscious, quickly get your fingers into the mouth and hook out the obstructing material from one side to the other until you are satisfied the airway is clear.

Keep checking that the airway remains clear. Check that the chest is rising and falling, thereby receiving oxygen. Talk to the patient calmly and clearly at all times. Continually reassure the casualty he or she is doing well.

Once the airway has been freely vented and the casualty is relatively stable, carry on with a primary survey by exposing more of the body to inspection.

Apply dressings

Check the victim with both hands. Gently roll the patient over and check the back methodically, and don't forget the armpits. You are looking for blood from other, less obvious wounds, so be sure to keep checking your hands for signs of blood. Essentially, you are looking for more holes to plug, more hemorrhaging that needs to be controlled.

It's important to know that all bleeding is not the same. There are, in fact, two types of bleeding: arterial from ruptured arteries, and venous from breached veins.

Arterial blood will spurt strongly and will be bright red in color because it is rich in oxygen, having been replenished by the lungs. Arterial blood needs to be controlled first because it pumps out at a fast rate.

Venous blood is dark red and it will ooze from tissue, not spurt like a fountain. Venous blood will not issue from wounds to the lungs.

In a military situation, you would use the pressure dressing in your kit. However, there are unlikely to be specialist field dressings at the scene of a terror attack, so you'll have to adapt and improvise.

For instance, folded clothing and duct tape make a passable pressure dressing. Apply the pad of clothing into the wound and wind the tape around a limb as tightly as possible.

When applying absorbent material, be brutal and fast. Push and twist and repeat until the cavity is full and you cannot pack any more into the wound. Stuff wounds with any packing vigorously.

To apply pressure, add whatever bandage or tape you have. Be thorough when applying the bandage, focusing on the wound area.

Wrap it around the middle, then the bottom, and finish at the top of the wound. Middle. Bottom. Top. If you don't cover the wound completely, you are wasting your time. If the dressing starts leaking, apply another one on top of the first. Do not remove the first dressing!

Chest wounds are a priority because uncontrolled air in the chest wall cavity is very dangerous. A gunshot wound or puncture from flying debris in the chest needs to be addressed quickly.

An improvised chest seal can be constructed with duct tape and plastic wrapping. Make a three-sided patch with the duct tape, cut a plastic bag to match the triangle, and tape it over the entry wound, leaving the center of one side of the triangle open.

This will allow air to blow out of the hole and not get sucked in. Then find the exit wound and use the duct tape to completely seal the gap. Blood is a natural adhesive; it coagulates very quickly, so you're just helping things along.

Once you have stabilized the casualties through the use of tourniquets and by freeing airways, once you've patched up other wounds, you can move on to the next most urgent patient identified in your triage.

Address other concerns

When all those in need of urgent, lifesaving intervention have been stabilized, you are then in a position to look at issues of infection prevention, as well as fractures, burns, and lacerations.

Be aware that bomb victims may be suffering from profound internal injuries caused by the shock wave. These require expert medical interventions beyond the capacity of first aid or even paramedics.

Bombs can also cause burns of varying degrees. These also require expert attention, but you can help by removing clothing from around the burned tissue. Be careful not pull any off the burn itself. Remove any jewelry, which otherwise would have to be cut off later because of swelling. Keep the patient warm to help with the effects of shock.

The more comfortable you can make your patients, the less problematic their prognosis is going to be in the long run. Bruising and pain are good indicators of strains or sprains, but those symptoms can also mask a hairline or complete fracture. The main giveaway with complicated fractures is deformity.

Strains and sprains can be made comfortable in seconds by applying, if available, an elasticized bandage. The pressure will support the injury until you reach help; keep the bandage wide, wrapping middle-bottom-top, middle-bottom-top.

Create a herringbone effect for maximum support. The victim may need to run on the injured limb again at a minute's notice, so do a good job first time.

If possible, record everything you have done to help the patient and any observations of his or her condition. You can do this with a pen and paper or record it onto your cell phone dictation app. It will help the medics speed up their assessment and treatment of the casualty.

You don't need to be exact, but help paramedics with a run-through of your first response treatment. For example, "I placed a tourniquet on twenty minutes ago. I patched a hole in the left side of his chest." It may help the professionals keep the patient alive.

The issue of tourniquets is so vital I want to return to it for a moment. When twenty schoolchildren and six adults were killed at the notorious Sandy Hook shooting in 2012, a group of prestigious US surgeons began an initiative known as the Hartford Consensus.

Its stated aim is that "no one should die from uncontrolled bleeding." To move toward this goal, a principle was established that all participants and bystanders in an event should be thought of as first responders.

The ultimate goal is to teach as many people as possible how to apply tourniquets. This important initiative is mirrored in the White House's Stop the Bleed campaign.

I heartily endorse the aims of these campaigns. Everyone should learn how to apply a tourniquet, just as everyone should learn CPR. Get involved! It's vital.

* * *

The first task in the aftermath is to ensure there is no further threat to the casualties.

The next priority is to assess or triage casualties to identify those who need the most urgent attention.

Bleeding is the critical factor to be addressed first, which means tourniquets and pressure pads. Learn these techniques. They may be vital at the scene of road accidents, too.

Chest wounds can also take a heavy toll, so learn the principles of a chest seal. Then fractures and cuts need to be addressed by splinting and cleaning.

Don't wait for paramedics. They may be held behind police lines for a considerable and crucial period of time.

Chapter Nine

SMARTPHONES AT THE ATTACK SCENE

In this chapter, I'll address a perplexing and complex aspect of active shooter events. It is one that's coming more and more to the forefront. It's the thorny question of digital technology and social media and its use at terror events—for good and for evil.

There are three general areas to consider. The first is the way victims use social media during an active shooter incident. The second is the use of social media by active shooters during the course of an attack—a growing and disturbing trend. Third is the use of social media by the general public not directly involved in the unfolding event. This involves those who may or may not have a view of the area under attack.

I've commented earlier on the near universal use of social media in developed societies. People are rarely more than a reach away from their smartphones and constantly interact with their chosen digital "communities."

Like everyone else I use digital technology, but I limit the way I use the most common of them: the smartphone. This is the ultimate in transportable technology. You can take it anywhere, but it will also insulate you from world around you if you let it.

Let me give you an example. It's common to see people walking down the street completely oblivious to their surroundings as they listen to their beats. And it's not uncommon to hear of the occasional person in this mode being so disconnected from reality that he or she steps off the sidewalk and gets struck by a vehicle.

This state of oblivion brought about by overuse of technology is the exact opposite of the state of awareness required to keep you safe and enhance your life experience. You cannot experience Situational Awareness from behind a set of earphones.

I know I'm swimming against the tide of modernity when I say this, but a growing body of opinion agrees with me. I hope you'll also agree and limit your smartphone usage to appropriate times and surroundings.

Let's look at the wider use of social media and see what role it plays in the activities of terrorists of all sorts.

Use by attackers

In one example, eighteen-year-old Ali Sonboly used Facebook to lure young victims to a shopping mall in Munich, Germany, in July 2016. Sonboly set up a fake account on Facebook posing as a pretty teenage girl named Selina.

Hours before the attack, he posted a message using this name saying: "Come today at four o'clock to McDonald's at the OEZ shopping mall. I am giving away anything you want as long as it's not too expensive."

Sonboly shot and killed nine people at that McDonald's table, including four teenagers who had come in response to his post.

The Pulse nightclub killer, twenty-nine-year-old Omar Mateen, was fond of posting preening selfies of himself on Facebook. These were a clue to his psychopathic narcissism.

But he'd also been using Facebook as a tool to try to identify the home addresses of Florida police officers. Evidently his Plan B was to assassinate a police officer and his family at home.

Of course, this sort of information is revealing and vital for the agents who investigate the motives behind an attack, and it's clear the authorities are working on ways of filtering social media to identify the profiles of a potential active shooter.

This is no easy task, and at this point I would make an appeal for everyone to be vigilant. If you see a pattern of thought developing in an online friend that points to a buildup of explosive violence, alert the authorities.

However, for victims caught up in the incident, there is a far more immediate and critical aspect to the perpetrator who is engaging in real-time social media negotiations with the authorities and statements to journalists.

It's quite simple:

While the assailant is talking or texting, he is not shooting!

While he's engaged in this way, he's not totally concentrating. This gives you the opportunity to quietly move to safer cover or to attack him. A shooter using his smartphone is comparable to the moment a shooter has to change magazines. His finger is not on the trigger. He is vulnerable.

Pulse shooter Omar Mateen engaged in numerous exchanges, speaking to police and journalists and posting on Facebook. These pauses from shooting might have offered opportunities to exploit. He was distracted by his engagement with social media.

This does not mean that those under the barrel of his rifle were in any position to capitalize on those moments, and it doesn't imply any criticism of them.

Other factors have to come into play during those minutes when the active shooter is engaged with social media or negotiators. They include the physical shape of the hostage and the knowledge of what actions are possible—precisely what this book is about.

Primary ISIS attackers appear to be the exceptions to the rules. By primary ISIS attackers, I mean those frontline fighters who are diverted to suicide attacks in Western cities. They waste no time on social media during an attack and stick assiduously to their task, which is to kill as many people as possible.

A feature of many ISIS high command–directed attacks, such as those in Paris and at Istanbul airport, is the absence of any lull through the use of social media. Neither is there any abatement of the killing through negotiations.

Many "high school" active-shooter events are driven by the attacker—who is often mentally ill—playing out violent fantasies. Negotiation is not generally part of the scenario, which may have been rehearsed many times in the mind of the assailant. However, this class of perpetrator may indulge in bizarre social media posting.

What about the use of social media by victims? I'm afraid there are lessons to be learned from some entirely understandable misjudgments, which have cost lives. This is precisely why I am writing this book. I want to prepare people for the worst. I want to give advice that could make all the difference.

Use by victims

It's perplexing but not surprising to learn the first instinct of some caught up in a terror event is not to duck or run. It's to tweet or to videorecord. I make no comment on whether this is a good or a bad thing.

Your cell phone or social media could be a lifesaving tool or, just as easily, a nail in your coffin. It all depends when and where you use it.

Some uses I wouldn't criticize, such as those occasions when people who are held hostage or badly wounded text or tweet their loved ones to say farewell and offer their love one last time.

However, the seconds and microseconds at the beginning of a terror incident are indispensable. Use that precious time to take cover, take stock of your situation, and go through the drills I've outlined in other chapters.

Do not be tempted to waste those irreplaceable moments for the sake of an upload. Try, if you can, to control your knee-jerk social media response. It may save your life and the lives of others.

There have been examples of people being wounded or killed while continuing to video active-shooter events. I would make a plea to people not to divert energy and waste seconds in filming or photographing.

I'm sure there is a syndrome at work here, which I first observed while on armed protection assignments with media crews in Iraq. Cameramen often seem to feel they're insulated from the realities of a battle by the prism of the lens.

I've watched them standing up in the midst of some serious incoming fire, apparently unconcerned with anything but the shot in the frame. They seem blissfully unaware that there's another type of shot, which could easily end it all.

It usually takes a moment of stark clarity, a round hitting nearby or the hand of someone like me dragging them down to cover, to bring them back to the moment.

I suspect an element of "lens syndrome" is at work in many who film with their cell phones. They seem to believe nothing can hurt them. It's as if they're not present at the scene; they're just watching things unfold from behind the "safety" of the lens.

The frame of a cell phone camera does not constitute a safe haven. It is definitely not a bulletproof screen. And so long as you are filming, you are wasting precious time that could be spent in doing the things I have outlined that will give you a chance of survival.

Having said that, there's no doubt this is a complex and multilayered problem. For instance, people who were relaxed and enjoying the evening at the Bataclan nightclub in Paris were already filming the band on their phones.

When the attack began, most of them thought the cracks of rounds being fired were merely sound effects on stage, just part of the atmosphere, not the reports of automatic weapons.

They had no idea they were under lethal attack until people began to fall dead and wounded around them. Some of those who were filming died, too. That's entirely understandable. It happened too quickly for them to react.

It was the same at the Pulse nightclub in Orlando. One young woman was already filming friends in the crowd. It seems she caught something unusual happening in the corner of her eye, turned to film it, and died a second later, still recording video footage. How was she to know? It was all over in instant.

In such cases, the victims could just as easily have been lifting drinks to their lips. It's just one of those tragic occurrences that are beyond the control of mere mortals.

My advice is to keep your cell phone in your pocket. Only take it out when you can use it, relatively safely, to change your situation or to alert and assist the authorities.

I'll now turn to the subject of the social media interaction of the general public who are acting as spectators on the sidelines of a terrorist event.

The fact of the matter is that social media exchanges during and following an active-shooter event can range from inaccurate and misleading to downright helpful to the perpetrator.

It's known that active shooters may take a pause during their activities to monitor chatter on sites such as Facebook or Twitter.

It's at this point the general public can be singularly unhelpful to the police and, crucially, to the victims and potential victims of an active shooter.

Use by the public

A case in point is an incident in San Diego, California, on November 4, 2015, when police were called to a domestic violence report. No sooner had officers arrived than they came under sustained fire from a high-powered rifle.

The officers retreated to set up a perimeter while the perpetrator found a commanding position, overlooking the neighborhood, on the roof of his apartment complex. He began firing at random into the community.

Police immediately tweeted a warning for residents to stay away from windows and a five-hour siege began.

But law enforcement was shocked by the stream of photographs being tweeted that showed police setting up firing positions in response to the shooter. In effect, members of the public were acting as forward spotters for the assailant, giving away police strategy and locations.

Outraged, the San Diego PD Officers Association tweeted: "Can you please stop showing officers positions & movements." Media, too, were asked to refrain from assisting the active shooter by broadcasting revealing, real-time information.

San Diego is not an isolated incident. The infamous Boston Marathon bombing in April 2013 led to a huge police manhunt for fugitive bomber Dzhokhar Tsarnaev.

This was obviously a potential active-shooter situation, and on April 19, with the hunt still very active, the Boston Police Department were at the end of their tether when they issued a media alert on Twitter.

It read: "Do not compromise officer safety by broadcasting tactical positions of homes being searched."

So-called people's journalists on social media, together with professional media outlets, had been tracking and publicizing every police move in the ongoing hunt for Tsarnaev and identifying the locations of police activity.

Obviously there are Fifth Amendment rights involved, but the question is not whether there is a right to film or photograph police activities. The question is whether it's prudent for a right-minded, responsible citizen to use that material in real time.

My advice for those on the edge of an unfolding terror event is simple. Do not use social media to provide a running commentary on what is happening within your overview.

Do not act as an agent for an active shooter who may well be monitoring social media for such information. Do not make yourself responsible for the lives of law enforcement officers and potential victims by the irresponsible use of social media. Cut out the chatter and online gossip.

Lives are at stake. Think before you tweet.

If war had been declared, and you were acting as a forward spotter for the enemy by passing on high-quality intelligence such as the positions of friendly forces—you would be shot as a spy!

* * *

Smartphones can be a lifesaver or a curse. Resist the modern knee-jerk response to use them to film or to take selfies during an attack. Once you are in reasonable cover, you may use them to alert and inform law enforcement, but do not risk all to do this. If you are hiding—for instance, in an office or a classroom, put your phone onto silent mode.

If you are observing an active event from neighboring properties, do not post or tweet anything on social media that might assist perpetrators with information or photographs on how law enforcement is deploying.

Chapter Ten

LESSONS TO BE LEARNED

In this chapter, we'll look at real-life terror attacks from around the globe. Most of them are notorious and infamous. At first this may appear to be a dismal list of murder and destruction. But in the midst of these tragedies there are shining examples of courage, hope, and resistance.

They graphically demonstrate that the lessons I've been teaching in this book aren't just theory or pie in the sky. Everything I'm trying to pass on in this book is backed up by the indomitable actions of individuals who took the fight to the bomber and the shooter.

I've split them up under different headings that reflect the various environments in which the attacks took place and describe the different challenges presented—for instance, between a school and a movie theater.

I know we can all take strength and courage from the examples of bravery and ingenuity drawn out in this chapter.

Streets and shopping malls

Attacks in shopping malls and streets generate just as much terror and confusion as anywhere. It's also true that high numbers of people have been killed in such locations. But they are the environments with the most possibilities of retaliation against active shooters.

Streetscapes and the multilevel warrens of a mall are ideal places to rapidly set up zones of resistance and disruption. Both are littered with potential weapons for those prepared to improvise and adapt.

In contrast to confined spaces such as movie theaters, they also provide more opportunity for escape and evasion and, although many people can fall victim to a killer, comparatively higher numbers survive.

I'll analyze a number of notorious incidents that illustrate the dilemmas and the potential for escape and counterattack.

Westgate Shopping Mall, Nairobi, Kenya; September 21, 2013

This was a large-scale attack by the Somali Islamist group al-Shabaab on the upscale mall favored by wealthy locals and Western tourists.

More than 170 people were wounded and 67 killed in the attack, which lasted for some hours. The gunmen escaped in the confusion.

Despite the apparent bungling of law enforcement and the high death toll, Westgate holds some important lessons for folk in the United States, not least because Kenya issues concealed-carry permits for handguns.

Carrying such a permit allowed a significant intervention to be made by a foreign national who was a resident in the country and working as a protection officer. This individual was a former member of the United Kingdom's elite Royal Marines Special Boat

Service—the equivalent of the Navy Seals—and he was carrying a semi-automatic pistol.

He was photographed shepherding a woman and a girl out of the mall with a pistol stuffed in his belt. They were believed to be his wife and daughter.

With his family safe, witnesses say he returned to the killing zone on a dozen separate forays to hustle over one hundred people to safety as he gave covering fire for their escape. This is the sort of formidable effort you'd expect from such a highly trained and motivated man.

Another concealed-carry hero in the Westgate was Abdul Haji, son of a former Kenyan defense minister. He'd received a text from his brother who was trapped inside the mall. Abdul rushed straight to the mall and used his pistol to give Red Cross workers cover as they retrieved the injured. He then continued on with them to a second-floor parking area where he teamed up with a group of five armed men, including three detectives, one of whom had been wounded in the stomach.

This ad hoc unit went from store to store rescuing people before returning to the ground floor, where they engaged the gunmen in a firefight.

Abdul Haji remained in the mall for three or four hours helping people escape from a restroom, a bank, and a burger restaurant. His brother also managed to escape.

The Westgate attack perfectly demonstrates how concealed-carry interventions can turn the tide and save lives.

ISIS Bombing; Ansbach Music Festival, Nuremburg, Germany; July 24, 2016

The instincts of one man saved scores of lives when terror struck at the summer music festival in Ansbach.

The eagle eyes of Pascal Bohm, a doorman at the event, perfectly encapsulate the lessons of Situational Awareness outlined in chapter two.

He spotted a suspicious character, Mohammad Daleel, who was a supposed Syrian refugee. A known fact is Daleel had fought with ISIS in Syria, had been wounded, and then treated in Germany.

Daleel had no sense of gratitude toward his host country and turned up at the event carrying a bomb in his backpack. However, he had not thought his plan through and forgot to buy a ticket.

Twenty-five-year-old Mr. Bohm didn't like the look of him and repeatedly turned Daleel away. Even so, the bomber continued to loiter around the entrance to the venue where two thousand five hundred people were enjoying the music.

In his own words, Pascal Bohm said, "Daleel seemed to hope I would leave my post and be replaced by someone who might allow him in. He kept phoning someone and had his hand on his ear to listen to the call. He kept staring at me nervously. Every movement seemed frantic, and he looked to see if he was being watched."

The doorman had read Daleel's body language absolutely correctly and in all probability would have alerted law enforcement had Daleel not left the festival entrance.

Mr. Bohm's suspicions proved all too correct when Daleel moved away from the entrance and exploded his backpack outside a nearby café. Daleel was killed, but mercifully only fifteen people were injured. The toll inside the crowded festival would have been far heavier.

There's little doubt Pascal Bohm's acute Situational Awareness spooked the bomber. Unnerved, Daleel moved away from the Target-Rich Environment to a far less bloody harvest. In fact, he was the only one to die.

Active Shooter; Tucson, Arizona; January 8, 2011

This notorious mass killing, which involved the prominent and well-loved US Representative Gabrielle Giffords, teaches us many lessons.

The congresswoman was holding an open forum, a constituent meeting in a supermarket parking lot at Casas Adobes in Tucson. As the meeting was underway, obsessive schizophrenic twenty-two-year-old Tucson resident Jared Lee Loughner drew a pistol and shot Representative Giffords in the head.

He began firing on the crowd around her, killing six people, including Chief Judge John Roll of the Federal District Court, one of the representative's staffers, and a nine-year-old girl, Christina-Taylor Green. Another twenty people were wounded.

At this point, a remarkable swarm attack unfolded to overwhelm Loughner and end the shooting. It began when an unidentified person smashed a folding chair over Loughner's back.

Next into the fray was seventy-four-year-old retired Army Colonel Bill Badger, who reacted with righteous fury and rushed the shooter after seeing little Christina-Taylor murdered.

As Badger charged, he was shot and wounded on the back of his head. But the old soldier's training had kicked in and he grabbed Loughner's wrist and pushed against his elbow joint. This forced him down to the ground while the shooter was attempting to change his ammunition clip.

At this point, another senior sprang into action when she heard someone shout, "Get his magazine!"

Patricia Maisch, sixty-one, didn't hesitate as she hustled the magazine out of Loughner's hand. His weapon, a Glock 19 9mm with an extended magazine, was torn away from him, too.

Bill Badger and an individual named Roger Salzgeber pinned

Loughner down. The elderly colonel used a choke hold on him while Patricia Maisch held his ankles.

At this point, a concealed carry-permit holder named Joe Zamudio, who'd heard the shots in a nearby store, ran to the sound of the commotion.

Zamudio's arrival on the scene provides us with some exemplars of people doing exactly the right thing at the right time. Zamudio had clicked off the safety on his 9mm semiauto handgun but kept the weapon out of sight in his pocket.

He saw Loughner on the ground with an older man standing above him. A gun was waving in the older man's hand, apparently advertising him as the shooter. Joe had his finger on the trigger and just milliseconds to make a decision, but some instinct told him to hold back for a moment.

Instead of shooting, he ran up to the struggling men and tried to snatch the gun from the older man's hand. It was then that bystanders shouted to him that the younger man on the ground was the real shooter.

Acutely aware he might have shot an innocent man, Joe later observed, quite rightly: "I could have done the wrong thing and hurt a lot more people."

Patricia Maisch's heroics continued when she rushed to get paper towels to apply pressure on Bill Badger's head wound. Nearby, another medical first response was saving Gabrielle Giffords's life. One of her interns, twenty-year-old Daniel Hernandez, saw there were multiple casualties.

In his own words, Hernandez said, "I went ahead and started doing the limited triage that I could with what I had."

Hernandez applied pressure to her wound and used smocks grabbed from the store as pressure bandages. During this "combat" treatment, the congresswoman was alert and able to squeeze his hand when he constantly asked if she could hear him.

It's a tribute to that instant medical first response, to all those who fought the killer, and to her own grit that Gabrielle Giffords fought to survive and recover. In 2016, she was on the podium at the Democratic National Congress making a stirring speech.

Loughner was sentenced to life imprisonment with no chance of parole in November 2012. Sadly, four years after the Tucson mass shooting, heroic Bill Badger died of pneumonia at the age of seventy-eight. God rest his brave soul.

What we learn from Tucson is the swarm or rush tactic can work extremely well as outlined in chapter five. We also see that the mechanics of a rush are spontaneous but it needs a human ignition to spark it off. In this case, it was an anonymous hero wielding a chair, and then old soldier Bill Badger took the initiative.

Tucson also tells us that prompt medical first response and triage as laid out in chapter eight works. No doubt Gabrielle Giffords's life was saved by the coolheaded work of her intern Daniel Hernandez. He and Patricia Maisch, who treated Bill Badger, improvised to effect the all-important stanching of blood. They embody the need for everyone to embrace the Stop the Bleed campaign. Everyone should learn the skills of CPR and the skills of pressure and how to make a tourniquet.

We can also learn from the actions of concealed-carry holder Joe Zamudio. His actions were textbook. Joe prepped his weapon for action but kept it discreet and out of sight, just as I advise in chapter seven. He kept his head and made the right call.

Truck Attack; Nice, France; Bastille Day, July 14, 2016

Around ten-thirty on the evening of July 14, an ISIS terrorist plowed a nineteen-ton truck through the crowds celebrating the national holiday on the promenade at Nice in southern France.

The terrorist drove on for nearly a mile at fifty miles per hour, smashing into people, killing or injuring them. He showed no mercy and smashed into several baby strollers in his path, murdering the infant occupants. In all, he killed 84 people and injured 202.

The perpetrator, Lahouaiej-Bouhlel, was shot dead by police at the end of his trail of destruction, and five accomplices have since been apprehended. He was believed to be high on the ISIS drug of choice, a powerful stimulant called Captagon.

You might think there's little anyone could do to stop a speeding truck short of shooting the driver. In fact, two audaciously brave, high-speed interventions finally stopped the terrorist.

The first was by motorcyclist Alexander Migues, who initially believed the truck was out of control before seeing the driver purposely steering toward victims. In a scene worthy of a film stuntman, Mr. Migues rode his bike alongside the passenger side of the truck, grabbed the door handle, and leapt the gap.

His bike fell under the wheels of the truck, dramatically slowing it. Alexander Migues dropped off the side of the truck when the terrorist fired a pistol at him. Someone else hurled his scooter under the wheels of the truck, too.

This allowed a female police officer to leap up and grapple the pistol in the driver's hand while two of her colleagues shot him.

Mr. Migues said afterwards, "I saw the truck run over this lady. It then came off the sidewalk and tried to run me over as well. Instinct took over. I can't even explain now how I started chasing the truck. I felt I had to do something."

I don't think there's any more I can add to this except to say that when the moment of peril comes, it brings out the courage and determination from the man and the woman.

Resorts

Resorts and holiday venues are another soft target favored by terrorists. A beach is a classic Target-Rich Environment and one that affords very little cover. If there are rocky outcrops or hotel balustrades nearby, try to get to them for cover.

Depressions in the beach can also afford effective dead ground cover as the kinetic energy of a bullet is quickly dissipated by sand. The lower portion of a beach umbrella can provide you with an effective spear.

In the case of a knife attack, you can use chairs to keep the attacker at bay and, if there are enough people, eventually corral him and bludgeon him.

Active Shooter; Sousse Beach Resort, Tunisia; June 26, 2015

Thirty-eight people, thirty of them British, were killed when ISIS gunman Seifeddine Rezgui attacked a beach resort and hotel complex popular with European tourists.

It appears that Rezgui, twenty-four, landed on the beach from a boat manned by accomplices. He then mingled with holidaymakers before he pulled a Kalashnikov assault rifle from a folded beach umbrella and opened fire. The killer, who was high on cocaine, also threw grenades.

There were some remarkable interventions during the prosecution of this attack. Hotel employees and beach traders formed a human chain across the beach and challenged Rezgui not to pass.

They were his fellow believers and, unwilling to kill them, the shooter turned away from scores of potential victims and attacked a nearby hotel. He rampaged through the building to emerge in a passageway alongside.

Behind him he had left thirty-eight murdered and scores of wounded after discharging four magazines indiscriminately. At this point, fifty-six-year-old Munsaf Mayyel, a local builder, was working on a rooftop above the passageway alongside the Imperial Marhaba Hotel.

Mr. Mayyel armed himself with handfuls of the ceramic and terra-cotta roof tiles he'd been working with and rained them down on the killer.

One struck Rezgui's head, stunning him and knocking him to the ground. The dazed killer got to his feet again, firing wildly into the air, trying to shoot his unseen assailant. This gave Tunisian police, waiting in cover at the end of the passageway, the opportunity to shoot and kill Rezgui. Later, Mr. Mayyel recalled he'd shouted: "You terrorist, you dog" at the gunman.

Builder Munsaf Mayyel's attack on the shooter from above was a perfect example of the disruption of a shooter's killing tempo. In this case, it also directly aided the neutralization of the terrorist by law enforcement.

Bombing and Active Shooting; Oslo, Norway; July 22, 2011

In many ways the so-called "lone wolf" attack by right-wing extremist Anders Breivik represents a perfect storm in terms of the cold-blooded planning and execution of a mass killing.

He first struck with a massive car bomb next to the tower block housing the prime minister's office in the Norwegian capital of Oslo. Eight people were killed and over two hundred received injuries with varying degrees of severity.

The authorities were left reeling by this first attack, but that was only the prelude to the main event. While police were determining where to start their investigation, Breivik was driving to a coastal island twenty-five miles to the northwest.

He was bound for a youth summer camp held by the ruling Labor Party on the island of Utoya. Wearing a homemade police officer's uniform and showing false ID, Breivik took the ferry to the island.

When he arrived, he told two summer camp directors he was undertaking a routine check after the recent bomb outrage in Oslo. Breivik shot them both at the start his rampage, which claimed 69 more lives and wounded 110 more people; 55 of them seriously.

He was shooting people on the island when he noticed people swimming across the lake to escape, so he started shooting at them in the water. Others wounded on the island played dead but he returned to finish them off.

People hid in undergrowth and in bathroom and shower blocks. Others hid on the rocky foreshore, some swimming to sea caves to hide. A large group of around fifty youngsters hid in the island's schoolhouse and survived when Breivik failed to shoot his way in through the heavy door.

Out of this hellish scene on the island emerges one of the most inspiring stories I have heard from an active shooting. Two of the youngsters were ethnic Chechen teenagers, resident in Norway.

They were Movsar Dzhamayev, seventeen, and Rustam Daudov, sixteen, and the events that day vividly reminded them of the dreadful war in their native land.

"I'd seen people being shot before in my country, when I was small, and I had flashbacks," said Dzhamayev.

But a truly remarkable cell phone conversation with his father gave him backbone and resolve. Past experience must have given his father a complete insight into the situation.

Dzhamayev said: "My dad told me, 'attack the perpetrator and do it properly.'"

Together with one of their friends, the teens armed themselves with rocks and the three of them returned to the scene where they saw Breivik shoot another youngster.

"We stood three meters from him and wanted to beat him, but then he shot one of our friends in the head. So we just threw the stones and ran for our lives," said Daudov.

At that point, they decided it was too difficult to take on Breivik in the open. Instead, they found a cave where they hid twenty-three children and stood guard outside. For good measure, Dzhamayev also rescued three drowning youngsters from the freezing lake.

There were heroic rescues by locals in boats who saved around 150 youngsters from the waters of the lake while Breivik was still active on the island.

When heavily armed law enforcement eventually arrived on the island, Breivik simply laid down his weapons and meekly surrendered. He is currently serving an indeterminate sentence after being convicted of the crimes.

Medical assistance was painfully slow in arriving on the island and many traumatic injuries were made worse by the lack of first-responder knowledge among survivors.

The lamentable failures of the police during the incident would take too long to list here. But one of their most unforgiveable failures followed the superb Situational Awareness of an Oslo citizen after the bombing in the city. This person spotted someone in a police uniform, pistol in hand, getting into an unmarked vehicle. It didn't look right and the witness called it in, even providing the police dispatcher with the license plate number.

It remained unread by police controllers for twenty minutes and the vehicle number wasn't put on an APB for a further two hours—by which time Breivik was already on the island killing people. That sort of initiative on the part of a vigilant member of the public, on the periphery of an incident, is precisely what the police need and precisely what I have advocated. It's a crying shame that in this case it was ignored.

The Utoya shooting, as with so many others, provides stark lessons about the need for Situational Awareness, as shown by the sadly ignored citizen, and for basic medical first response.

But for me the story of the two Chechen teens encapsulates much of the ethos of this book. I can only imagine what it took for the father of young Dzhamayev to tell his son to "take the shooter on and do it properly."

Schools

Of all places, schools and colleges are the most poignantly tragic scenes of mass shootings—no more so than elementary schools where parents entrust their little ones to a safe environment.

The plain truth is if an active shooter breaches the security of a school, the outcome will be devastating. What we see are some young lives ended and many more ruined physically or emotionally.

In a few instances, young children do something heroic even though they will barely understand the concept. Ultimately, teachers will be their shields, and time after time we see them emerge as beacons of courage and selfless humanity. All too often, teachers expose themselves to terror and lay down their lives to protect their young charges.

In high schools and colleges, students themselves can and will engage in their own defense. This is especially true where they've been given the basic knowledge to group together and change from a defensive to an attacking posture.

They, too, are able to help with vital medical first response. Below, I've looked at three attacks on schools and drawn the lessons to be learned from them.

Active Shooter; Dunblane Junior School, Scotland, United Kingdom; March 13, 1996

A cold Scottish morning witnessed forty-three-year-old "loser" Thomas Hamilton leaving his home in the city of Stirling to drive the five miles to the village of Dunblane. When he arrived at the village school, at about nine thirty in the morning, he took out a pair of pliers and severed the telephone cables at the base of a pole, effectively cutting off communications.

Hamilton then strolled across a parking lot and into the school at an entrance near the gymnasium. He walked in with four legally held handguns, two 9mm Browning HP pistols and two Smith and Wesson .357 revolvers, and began shooting at the first grade pupils.

Twenty-eight pupils and three members of staff were in the room when he walked in, brandishing a pistol. He was immediately confronted by teacher Eileen Harrild, and he opened fire.

He had wounded her, but her brave intervention spooked Hamilton, who fired randomly around the room. Eileen Harrild, although shot three times in the arm and chest, still managed to shepherd several injured children into a storeroom.

At this point, another teacher, Gwen Mayor, was shot and killed instantly. The other adult present, Mary Blake, a supervisory assistant, was hit in the head and both legs. She, too, managed to usher several children into the store cupboard.

CSI officers later worked out that within a few steps Hamilton had fired twenty-nine shots, killing one child and injuring several more. The killer then went to the other end of the gym before turning to discharge sixteen shots at point-blank range into a group of children previously wounded from his earlier rounds.

Hamilton continued firing in haphazard directions at random human targets as he left the gym through the fire exit into the cloakroom of the library. Teacher Catherine Gordon was in an adjacent classroom and told her class to get onto the floor just as Hamilton fired nine shots into the room.

Bullets struck books and a chair where a pupil had been sitting only an instant before. Catherine Gordon's quick thinking doubtlessly saved several of the children in her charge from death or serious wounds.

Hamilton may have had some realization of what he'd done. Despite the fact he still had over seven hundred rounds of ammunition with him, he walked back into the gym and shot himself. He had murdered sixteen children and teachers and wounded another sixteen—all in the space of three or four minutes.

Obviously, the quick thinking and selfless courage of the teachers at this little village school is an example to one and all. They laid their lives on the line and were true heroines.

But Dunblane Junior School also provides us all with another hero. Waiting to enter the gymnasium for the next lesson that fateful morning was an eleven-year-old lad named Andy Murray.

In 2016, the same Andy Murray, transformed into a twenty-nine-year-old tennis superstar, won his second Wimbledon Tennis Championship and his second Olympic gold medal.

In an emotional interview, his only one about the day so many of his school friends were murdered, he talked about having given something back to his home village. He hoped he'd given back hope and pride.

Society often discusses the implications of Post-Traumatic Stress Disorder, which can tragically result from active shooter incidents and bombings. But I like to think of the Dunblane story and Andy Murray's role in it as a parable of hope. It is part of the human condition that we strive to survive and achieve against all the odds.

Active Shooter; Sandy Hook Elementary School, Newtown, Connecticut; December 14, 2012

Numerous investigations have failed to learn Adam Lanza's motive for the murder of twenty children, aged six and seven, together with six adults at the Sandy Hook Elementary School.

Twenty-year-old Lanza first murdered his mother Nancy at their home in the community of Newtown. He then went on to establish the gruesome record of the deadliest school shooting in US history.

Perhaps Lanza had some twisted wish to make himself a historical figure. For my part, I prefer to concentrate on the quick-thinking heroes who thwarted him, some of whom remain anonymous to this day at their own insistence.

The first was an individual who heard shots fired and immediately turned on the school intercom broadcasting the sound of shooting as a warning to staff.

Twenty-six lives were coldly, almost casually snuffed out. But how many more might have died were it not for that timely alert of the lethal danger stalking the school corridors? Whoever flipped that switch set off a warning system and, as I constantly point out, seconds save lives during active-shooter events.

Sandy Hook teacher Theodore Varga, who was present at the time, summed it up graphically: "Whoever did that saved a lot of people. Everyone in the school was listening to the terror that was transpiring."

This was a brilliant and unusual example of disruption of a killer's pattern of attack as I outlined in chapter four. Another anonymous hero—who knows . . . it may have been the same person—was a school custodian who ran from classroom to classroom completely ignoring his own safety.

According to Theodore Varga, this courageous individual was a hero who called out: "Guys! Get down! Hide!"

Forty-seven-year-old school principal Dawn Hochsprung ran out of a meeting to confront Lanza. Ordering other staff to keep behind her, she put herself in the line of fire and rushed the killer. Her gallantry cost her life.

She epitomizes the do-or-die courage I talk about when I discuss confronting and attacking shooters in chapter five.

After murdering the principal, Lanza turned to the meeting room where other staff were hiding. The door to the room had no lock, so a teacher held it shut with the weight of her body. Frustrated at his inability to force the door open, Lanza shot through the door, wounding the anonymous teacher in the leg and arm. Still, she held it closed, refusing to give way. Such heroics inspire the philosophy of this book.

Soon after, first grade teacher Victoria Leigh Soto, aged twenty-seven, was shot in her classroom after misleading Lanza by telling him her students were in the gym. However, some of her terrified charges broke cover and Lanza began shooting them, too. With no hesitation Victoria threw herself between the killer and the children, sacrificing her life for them.

Hers was a standout moment of gallantry in a day filled with courage. She was posthumously awarded the Presidential Citizens Medal. Victoria Leigh Soto gave her life to save the children in her charge while she disrupted the shooter's rhythm and bought precious seconds for others.

Another first grade teacher, Kaitlin Roig-DeBellis, ordered her fifteen students into a tiny children's restroom, just three feet by four feet. It was so small she stacked children on top of the cistern.

When law enforcement arrived, she refused to open the door and they had to find a key to free the class, which had survived.

That was absolutely the correct thing to do. Wait for officers to slide their ID under the door. Otherwise, assume it's the shooter trying to fool you.

Music teacher Maryrose Kristopik improvised when she hid twenty students in various closets and in the recesses of instruments such as xylophones and drums to disguise their hiding places. She then stubbornly held on to the door handle to prevent entry while the shooter kept banging on the door screaming: "Let me in! Let me in!"

Time and again, teachers at Sandy Hook showed their utter determination to confound the shooter's intentions, even though they were limited in escape and evasion options by their responsibility for very young children.

The shooting at Sandy Hook ended after five minutes when Lanza shot himself with his Glock pistol. During those five minutes, some heroes survived while others died.

All those who died did so showing they weren't sheep and they didn't go easily to the slaughter.

Active Shooting and Bombing; Columbine High School, Columbine, Colorado; April 20, 1999

The Columbine High massacre stands out because of the elaborate and coordinated plans hatched by two senior students to wreak havoc at their own school. Central to their plot was the mass shooting. However, Eric Harris and Dylan Klebold also built many makeshift bombs to divert officers away from their murderous enterprise.

By the time they committed suicide on campus, they had murdered twelve students and a teacher and wounded twenty-four others. The best handle investigators could get on their motives came from their journals, where they expressed low self-esteem and a wish to rival the Oklahoma City bombing and other outrages for infamy.

Put simply, they wanted to go out with a bang—and, motivated by jealousy, to take as many school athletes with them as possible. They targeted "jocks" from the outset. Realizing this, one unnamed girl jumped onto a youth with a sports logo on his T-shirt to hide the logo from the killers.

Dave Sanders, the one teacher who was murdered, saved the lives of several students, pulling them out of the line of fire and dragging one wounded boy to cover so he wouldn't be shot again. He continued these rescue attempts until he was shot himself and told students tending him: "Tell my daughter I love her."

Daniel Lee Rohrbough, fifteen, was another posthumous hero who held open a door for his classmates to flee through and was shot and killed before he could escape himself. Two janitors, Jon Curtis and Jay Gallentine, also acted heroically, putting themselves in harm's way in the cafeteria to bundle students into cover.

Crucially, Adam Foss, an eighteen-year-old senior, was in the second-floor choir room with sixty other students as the gunmen were advancing in their direction. He barked out an order to the others to get into an adjacent office, and when some froze he organized a team of older youths to physically move them to safety. Once they were all secure inside, he directed the building of a makeshift barricade.

Something must be in the Foss genes because in another part of the school, Adam's twin brother Nick calmly triaged two wounded classmates. He concluded there was nothing he could do for them. Then he looked up right into the barrel of a shotgun as it fired, but somehow the cloud of pellets missed him. Nick went on to rescue a cook and several students who he led to safety.

Quick-thinking science teacher Kent Friesen pulled students into a classroom and removed the bulbs from the emergency lights to create a dark zone to confound the shooters. Then he collected an arsenal of dry chemical fire extinguishers to attack the killers should they try to enter. And so it went on with teachers, students, and two fire department paramedics making the list of those who risked their own lives to save others.

Columbine shows us that people thinking on their feet can disrupt the rhythm and tempo of a shooting and make time for others to escape. Kent Friesen worked it out for himself. Fire extinguishers are a prime weapon.

Movie theaters

This is a desperate environment when under attack, with a concentration of victims lined up in the rows of seats like ducks at a fairground shooting gallery. The darkness also provides the shooter with concealment before he starts killing the occupants.

The best advice is to hunker down in the seating until you've worked out where the shooter is and which way he's moving. From a commanding position on the main aisle, a shooter can see those trying to escape through the emergency exits and will typically open fire on them.

This is definitely a situation where you should try to rush a shooter once you are in his Six.

Active Shooter; Movie Theater, Aurora, Colorado; July 20, 2012

The Century 16 Theater was hosting a midnight screening of *Batman: The Dark Knight Rises* when a gunman in tactical clothing threw tear gas canisters into the audience and used a variety of weapons to fire into the crowd.

Twelve people were killed and seventy injured by James Eagan Holmes who, uncommonly, survived. Dressed like a SWAT officer, he was arrested in his car outside the theater.

The case led to controversy because Century 16 theaters had a "no guns" policy, prompting many to argue that a concealed carrier might have ended the carnage. In August 2015, Holmes was given twelve life sentences. He has no possibility of parole.

As in all such shootings, Aurora presents a depressing prospect with innocent lives extinguished on what should have been a pleasant evening's entertainment. But there are lessons to be learned.

The killer bought a ticket but then slipped out the emergency exit, jamming it open in order to retrieve weapons from his car. He reentered the theater and walked up the aisle, between the rows of seating, shooting at those closest to him. Whenever he noticed fleeing people near the emergency exit, he shot them.

Best estimates are the shooting lasted no more than three minutes, during which time fifty to sixty shots were fired. Upon their swift arrival, police were able to identify Holmes as the shooter, not as the SWAT officer of his disguise, and he was detained.

Jennifer Seeger described how Holmes entered through the emergency exit. Her seat was one of the first he passed and his gun came close to her. Holmes passed her by on his way up the aisle and she started telling people they needed to crawl out using the seating for concealment.

Jennifer Seeger quickly recognized the dangerous reality of row after row of confining seats—no point bunching up behind each other. Get down and crawl out.

Active Shooter; Movie Theater, Lafayette, Louisiana; July 23, 2015

Fifty-nine-year-old John Houser, sometime law student, bar owner, and drifter, with complex mental health and personality issues, pulled out a pistol and opened fire on the audience at a matinee showing of the movie *Trainwreck*.

Of the one hundred or so people in the auditorium, two were murdered and nine were wounded, some with serious and life-changing injuries. Like the Aurora cinema shooting, this incident took place in a Grand 16 theater.

Houser's first victims were two people sitting in the row directly in front of him. He then fired thirteen more rounds, reloading once. Houser left the theater through a side exit and headed for his vehicle. But, on hearing police sirens, he went back inside and fired three more shots at moviegoers. He then shot himself.

Two police officers were already on duty within the environs of the theater complex, but by the time they'd rushed to the auditorium—within a couple of minutes—it was all over and Houser lay dead with his victims. However, once again, we have accounts of game-changing heroics among the innocents. School librarian Jena Meaux was with her friend and colleague Ali Martin, an English teacher, when the shooting began.

Jena threw herself over Ali to save her from the shots and took a bullet in her own leg. Ali Martin, who'd also been shot in the leg, instantly leaped up and pressed the fire alarm, which alerted the police officers already patrolling the complex.

Crucially, according to colleagues, both women testified their school lockdown training had kicked in instantly. One colleague said Ali had even checked out where the fire alarms were earlier.

Ali knew that triggering the alarm would lead to the rest of the complex being evacuated in case the shooter moved out of the auditorium he'd already shot up. Said the colleague: "She was knowledgeable enough even after being shot to do that."

Personally, I always choose my seat carefully, not just in a movie theater, but in any public place. When watching a movie, I prefer to have a seat on the aisle, which gives me time and space to react should I need to. Remember that Situational Awareness is always important, so make a note of the exits, the fire alarms, and the extinguishers before the lights dim. Ali Martin did.

Nightclubs and other venues

A nightclub is yet another Target-Rich Environment with the added advantage, for the perpetrator, of loud music, disorienting lights, and a crowd possibly under the influence of drink or drugs.

Follow the rules. Get out of the Ten to Two and, if possible, get into the shooter's Six. Grab a bottle or a fire extinguisher. Your best chance will be to lead a swarm over him from his Six. Remember to be savage.

Active Shooting; Pulse Nightclub, Orlando, Florida; June 11, 2016

The attack on the Pulse nightclub by twenty-nine-year-old security guard Omar Mateen was the worst terror attack in the United States since 9/11 and took the shameful record for the most people murdered by an active shooter in the nation.

Forty-nine people were killed and fifty-three were wounded by Mateen, an ISIS fanatic, who was shot dead by officers of the Orlando Police Department after a three-hour standoff. The severity of the incident and its unusually extended time frame provide us with many lessons.

Three police officers first exchanged fire with Mateen as he approached and entered the nightclub, which allowed dozens to escape. However, Mateen was still able to take control of the club where he ended up killing at will for about twenty minutes.

The killing abated when Mateen himself contacted law enforcement and a local radio station to "negotiate." He was also active on social media. This went on for two hours, during which time

Mateen continued to murder people from time to time, on a whim. The siege ended when police breached a wall with an armored vehicle and Mateen was shot.

During the shooting, club bouncer Imran Yousuf, a twenty-year-old former US Marine who'd served in Afghanistan, saved dozens of lives. There was a rush to the back of the club where people were "sardine packed." Imran knew of a door that was accessible but out of sight. He took the risk and jumped into the firing zone to open the latch and liberate around seventy potential victims.

Club patron Joshua McGill, a nursing student, was taking cover in the parking lot when he saw bartender Rodney Sumter stumbling about and obviously bleeding out. He pulled him into cover and used his shirt to stanch blood from two gunshot wounds in Rodney's arms. But there was a third, major wound in his back.

McGill managed to get the bartender to a police vehicle and lay on his back, with Rodney on top of him, holding pressure on the back wound during the life-saving ride to hospital.

Two posthumous heroes were Edward Sotomayor Jr., thirty-four, who died while shielding his boyfriend from the bullets, and Brenda Lee Marquez McCool, who took a bullet to save her twenty-one-year-old son.

Heroism aside, major lessons are to be gained from the Pulse massacre. The first is that you can only depend on yourself. After the initial interventions by individual officers, it took law enforcement nearly three hours to storm the building.

It follows that you'll have to rely on your own wits and basic medical skills until professional help arrives. At times like these, you will rue the day if you never learned how to tourniquet a bleed out or administer basic treatment for a sucking chest wound.

Learn these techniques today. Keep them in your locker of knowledge until the day you need them.

It appears there were chances to swarm the killer but they were missed. I suspect a lack of knowledge lay behind this. Swarm sooner, rather than later, in a crowded environment.

Active Shooters; Bataclan Nightclub, Paris, France; November 13, 2015

Three ISIS gunmen attacked this famous Paris music venue while US rock group Eagles of Death Metal were playing. It was one of a series of coordinated attacks across the French capital that night.

Eighty-nine people were murdered and over two hundred were wounded in the club. A total of 130 were killed at locations across Paris that night. Two of the shooters blew themselves up with suicide belts. A third assailant was shot dead by police.

In the midst of the carnage there were some heroes who took calculated risks against the killers. One was a security guard known only as Didi who, according to survivors, saved about four or five hundred people.

When the shooters burst past him into the club, he followed them and opened emergency doors behind them, allowing people to escape. He came out of the club, realized more exits were needed, and returned to open more.

When the gunmen stopped to reload, Didi jumped up and called on people to follow him out. When Didi realized a killer was waiting to shoot those leaving through the exits, he rallied people again and led them to a nearby apartment block.

Didi made that run through the fire zone several more times to get people to safety. Survivors say he was "calm and in charge" and filled them with confidence.

Didi used his knowledge of the area, his Situational Awareness, and a calm, calculating nature to confound the terrorists in their aim of maximum destruction. Combined with his deep sense of humanity, those attributes saved many lives.

Active Shooters; Inland Regional Center, San Bernardino, California; December 2, 2015

Colleagues who gathered at the County Department of Public Health training event and Christmas party had no idea of the true nature of Syed Rizwan Farook and his wife Tashfeen Malik.

About eighty employees were in the rented banquet hall on Waterman Avenue at about ten thirty in the morning when Farook posed for photos with them and then slipped away, leaving a backpack on a table.

He returned a minute before midday, this time with his wife. They arrived as ISIS terrorists, wearing ski masks and black tactical vests and bearing semiautomatic rifles and pistols.

They opened fire indiscriminately on the crowd, discharging around seventy-five bullets in a frenetic burst of violence lasting four minutes. Fourteen people died during the planned attack and twenty-two were seriously injured. Almost all the victims were shot in the back.

At some point during this four-minute killing spree, Tashfeen Malik posted a pledge of bay'ah, or allegiance, to the leader of ISIS on social media. Then, unusually for a mass shooting, the killers fled the scene rather than commit suicide or continue firing until brought down by officers.

When they fled, the couple left behind three explosive pipe-bomb devices—ironically connected by Christmas lights—inside the backpack to attack first responders. They were clumsily constructed and failed to ignite.

It's probable that the couple, who had amassed a considerable armory at their home, believed they wouldn't be identified and would be able regroup and formulate more attacks. However, Farook's surviving coworkers did recognize him from his voice, build, and other characteristics and reported their suspicions to law enforcement.

Having a positive identification allowed officers to quickly discover that Farook had rented a black Ford SUV, which was spotted leaving a town house in Redlands close to the couple's home address. A considerable collection of weapons and bombs was later discovered at this property, which was rented by Farook and Malik as their terror base.

The vehicle was pursued onto the freeway and a mobile gun battle ensued, with the terrorists firing from the rear window of the SUV for several blocks. This continued until Farook stopped and exited the vehicle, and the couple continued to exchange fire with the police.

An officer came onto Farook outside his Ten to Two and wounded him, allowing others to outflank him and then kill him. His wife was shot minutes later inside the vehicle. This final shootout involved more than twenty officers who fired 380 rounds at the perpetrators.

There were individual acts of courage at San Bernardino, notably Shannon Johnson's selfless sacrifice when he shielded twenty-seven-year-old colleague Denise Peraza and told her: "I got you."

Those were his last words as he died in the hail of bullets fired by the terrorists. There were also many acts of gallantry under fire by law enforcement that shouldn't be forgotten, even though this book is primarily focused on unarmed civilians.

The initial attack was a lightning assault at point-blank range. Uncharacteristically, it was disengaged just as suddenly as it had begun. There was no time for victims to escape, evade, or confront the perpetrators.

Lessons are to be learned though. First, San Bernardino underscored the cold-blooded nature of fanaticism. When Farook and Malik left home that morning, they left behind their baby daughter, saying they were going to a medical appointment. Such a mind-set is merciless, as I have impressed on readers from the start.

Other issues relate to the digital environment we live in. The couple felt obligated to post their loyalty to the ISIS cause on Facebook. This is an increasingly followed ritual or observance during the passage of terrorist-inspired active shooter events as discussed in chapter nine.

In this case, it made no material difference to the outcome. However, you may find yourself in a situation where a shooter is using his or her cell phone on social media. This is a distraction to the perpetrator and a moment of vulnerability. It is a moment, such as reloading, which gives him pause and gives you an opportunity to attack.

Another issue relates to Farook's iPhone which, a year after the shooting, the FBI was still unable to break into. Apple was called upon to assist but declined to do so. A legal wrangle between the FBI and Apple ensued but this ended when the agency employed professional hackers to bust into the phone.

If an active shooter takes time from the attack to post on social media, be prepared to take advantage of the distraction.

Trains and planes

Trains and planes are basically capsules on the move. Their speed and—certainly in the case of an aircraft—their fragility make them so susceptible to attack.

Passengers are corseted into the confines of the capsule and there is little room for movement. This is perfect for the terrorist hell-bent on destruction, as we've learned all too tragically.

Acquiring defensive weapons, especially in the case of an aircraft, is difficult because of security vetting and the fact that everything is bolted down for safety.

The best defense in a plane or train is to remember that the shooter or hijacker is equally hemmed in for space. This renders him vulnerable to counterattack from a rush or swarm. Don't forget about using your book bag or hot drinks as improvised weapons. And whatever you do, in this case, do it sooner rather than later.

Active Shooter; Thalys Train, Pas-de-Calais, France; August 21, 2015

Passengers on the regular service from Amsterdam to Paris were attacked by a lone ISIS terrorist near the town of Oignes on the Belgian border.

However, this active shooter hadn't counted on the reaction of a group of passengers—principally an unlikely quartet of two off-duty US servicemen in transit with a friend, and a British pensioner with a bulldog spirit.

The perpetrator was Ayoub El Khazzani, a Moroccan national armed with an assault rifle and nine magazines of ammunition. He also carried a pistol, a knife, and a bottle of gasoline.

He prepared himself for the attack in the train restroom, but as he emerged with his rifle, a twenty-eight-year-old Frenchman was first to attack him, albeit unsuccessfully. A second Frenchman attempted to wrest the rifle from him but was shot through the neck and seriously wounded.

Three Americans, Airman First Class Spencer Stone and civilian Anthony Sadler, both twenty-three, and Specialist Alek Skarlatos, twenty-two, then joined the attack.

Stone, first into the fray, was slashed multiple times and had his finger nearly severed off with a blade. Skarlatos seized the assailant's rifle and beat him with it. The British passenger, Chris Norman, sixty-two, rushed in to hold the assailant down as Skarlatos beat him.

They tied up the terrorist and helped the injured French passenger who was spurting blood from his neck. Stone, a medic, stuck two fingers into the wound and compressed an artery until the bleeding stopped.

After the attack, Chris Norman and the three young Americans were showered with honors, including France's highest award, the Legion D' Honneur. The assailant was jailed.

The swarm response to this active shooter event on a train by the quick-witted passengers was outstanding. It's no surprise that young US servicemen reacted with military determination, but the action of the untrained Englishman was gutsy and determined, too.

Once again, I draw your attention to the lifesaving knowledge of how to deal with a bleed. This is a vital skill. It saves lives—learn it.

Flight 93; September 11, 2001.

It's a date the world will never forget, the day when four commercial aircraft were hijacked and used to strike at the very heart of the United States. Three of those aircraft hit their intended targets: the Twin Towers and the Pentagon. But thanks to the sheer guts and courage of the passengers on board Flight 93, the fourth aircraft couldn't strike a blow.

Doubtless al-Qaeda meant the aircraft to be flown straight into another icon of democracy; security services believe the White House itself and Capitol Hill were likely targets.

Instead, it crashed into the Pennsylvania countryside, killing all those on board but thwarting the sinister cause of al-Qaeda. Almost three thousand people lost their lives on 9/11, but the raw courage of the crew and passengers of Flight 93 doubtless prevented countless more casualties.

Flight 93 was a regular nonstop United Airlines flight scheduled from Newark, New Jersey, to San Francisco, California. That morning it was carrying seven crew and thirty-three passengers. Four hijackers had also boarded the plane with hidden knives and box cutters.

Takeoff was delayed by air traffic control; this disrupted the terrorists' schedule and they didn't take over the aircraft until forty minutes into the flight.

By then, warnings about possible attacks on flight decks were being transmitted, but Flight 93's cockpit had been taken over just two minutes after Captain Jason Dahl had requested clarification of these alerts.

Air Traffic Control heard sounds of fighting and two Mayday calls from the cockpit before terrorist leader Ziad Jarrah was heard ordering passengers to sit in the back of the plane. He threatened them with a bomb, which didn't exist.

First-class flight attendant Debbie Welsh was heard struggling with the hijackers before being killed. This is followed by one of the hijackers saying in Arabic: "Everything is fine. I finished."

Sometime during the fight, Captain Dahl and his copilot First Officer Homer put the craft on autopilot heading west and patched the flight deck onto the announcement setting to alert passengers and crew about the situation.

It took Ziad Jarrah some time to reset the autopilot with the dying captain courageously refusing to help. Eventually, Jarrah brought the plane back around to the east on a heading for Washington, DC. Huddled in the back of the plane, the passengers and crew of made a series of calls on cell phones and the in-flight Airfones.

Passengers and crew told family and the authorities about their perilous situation and learned of the three other aircraft that had been hijacked and flown into major targets. A brief, whispered discussion about their situation followed and a vote was taken. They decided to fight back. Thomas Burnett Jr. called his wife and told her: "I know we're all going to die. There's three of us who are going to do something about it. I love you, honey."

Flight attendant Sandy Bradshaw told her husband she was filling pitchers with scalding water to use against the hijackers. Her last words: "Everyone's running to first class. I've got to go. Bye."

Todd Beamer was on an open line to operator Lisa Jefferson and told her that passengers planned to jump the hijackers and fly the plane into the ground to protect national targets. He recited the Lord's Prayer and Psalm 23 with Jefferson, while others joined in. Then he said: "If I don't make it, please call my family and let them know how much I love them."

After this, Jefferson heard muffled voices and Beamer clearly answering: "Are you ready? Okay. Let's roll." That was the signal, and according to the in-flight voice recorder the passengers and crew aboard Flight 93 began their counterattack at 9:57 a.m.

Honor to them.

Elizabeth Wainio called her stepmother and told her: "They're getting ready to break into the cockpit. I have to go. I love you. Good-bye."

Jarrah is heard asking: "Is there something? A fight? They want to get in here. Hold, hold from the inside. Hold from the inside. Hold!" The terrorist pilot began rolling and pitching the aircraft in a bid to throw the counterattackers off their feet.

The cockpit voice recorder captured the sounds of crashing, screaming, and the shattering of glass and plates. Three times in a period of five seconds there were shouts of pain or distress from a hijacker outside the cockpit.

Jarrah stabilized and asked: "Is that it? Shall we finish it off?" Another terrorist answered: "No. Not yet. When they all come, we finish it off."

A passenger called out: "In the cockpit. If we don't, we'll die."

Another passenger yelled: "Roll it!" That may have been a reference to using a food trolley as a battering ram on the flight deck door.

It's pretty certain the passengers killed the hijacker guarding the door and breached through to the flight deck where a fight for control of the plane took place. As Jarrah began to put the aircraft down, the passengers continued their assault and the flight recorder captured a struggle going on for control of the con. Fearing they'd be overcome, the terrorists decided to crash the plane. Flight 93 picked up speed as it rolled over and nosedived into the ground at Stonycreek, Pennsylvania, about twenty minutes' air time from Washington, DC.

Their plan to attack the heart of democracy had been thwarted by a combined and sustained counterattack by the crew and passengers of the aircraft. The crash site is known as "Sacred Ground" and is a part of the Flight 93 National Memorial. That's a fitting memorial indeed, but what better legacy could they have than the story of their courage echoing through history?

The actions of the heroes of Flight 93 speak for themselves. I offer no analysis of this event except to say:

They didn't go to the slaughter like sheep. They were lions roaring their defiance.

Be a hero just like them!